ONE HOUR CRAFT

ONE HOUR CRAFT

To Amelia, my most beautiful creation.

First published in Great Britain in 2009 by
A & C Black Publishers Limited
36 Soho Square
London W1D 3QY
www.acblack.com

ISBN: 978-0-7136-8836-8

CIP Catalogue records for this book are available from the British Library and
the U.S. Library of Congress.

Commissioning editor: Susan James
Managing Editor: Sophie Page
Designer: Jo Tapper
Proof reader: Jo Waters

This book is produced using paper that is made from wood grown in managed,
sustainable forests. It is natural, renewable and recyclable. The logging and
manufacturing processes conform to the environmental regulations of the country of
origin.

Printed and bound in China

Acknowledgements

I would like to gratefully acknowledge the wonderful support and help I have received when writing this book. I was truly humbled by the number of family and friends who walked beside me as I completed the manuscript and the many hours spent creating and photographing.

Amelia: Thank you for all the help you gave me. Thank you for your patience when I spent so much time away from you. Thank you for your smiles, enthusiasm about my project and great ideas. Thanks for all the fetching, holding up and writing you did. You are the best little helper in the world and I could not have written the book without you. I love you.

Michael: Your patience was immeasurable. Thank you for the many hours you gave to photo shoots and editing. And all the nights spent in front of a computer. I am very grateful for your tenacity. Thank you also for your encouragement.

Emma: Like always, you are by my side, encouraging me and stunning me with your brilliant skills as a seamstress. I feel very blessed to have you as my twin sister!

Mum: You are the one who taught me to create. Thanks for teaching us all to sew and use our hands. Thanks for all the knowledge imparted throughout the process of writing this book. You are my sewing guru and I will always be in awe of your unendingly creative and skilful hands.

Dad: Thanks for the listening ear for all my complaints. Thanks also for the brilliant photography and helpful tips.

Kate: There is no other person in the world who makes me laugh like you do. You are a creative goddess who generously shares all you know with anyone who wants to listen. Thanks so much for your time helping with the Clay chapter and editing. Carnarvon was worth it, if only to meet a friend like you.

My creative girl posse: Thanks to the many creative women who have helped me along the way. Thanks Rachael for the graphic design help, Sharon for the help with the jewellery and all the creative ladies on the internet who inspire me everyday.

Contents

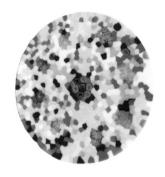

Introduction

Hi, I am Maria, the author of One Hour Craft. This book has been written for all sorts of different people; those with little time on their hands like professional women and mothers, or those who are dying to start crafting but have felt too intimidated or just those who are looking for quick inspiration. This book will help you take little steps towards a big creative future. If you don't have an hour, break the time down further and give up fifteen minutes a day for four days to create a fabulous necklace, a bag or some gorgeous soaps.

One Hour Craft has also been written for those of you who have been crafting for a long time and just want a shake up. I recently taught a class to a friend who is a completely amazing quilter. She used to spend hours upon hours making ornate quilts. But after many years she had become a little tired of committing to such long time periods to create her quilts. At the end of the One Hour Craft workshop she had produced a gorgeous, practical bag. She said it was enough to motivate her to begin crafting again, even though her life is very full of other commitments.

In this book, I have included a huge variety of crafts to spark your interest in many different areas and encourage you to try something new.

I have also included hot tips and helpful ideas to get you to start to think creatively. Take this raw material I have given you, and make it your own. I encourage you to step out and use bold and different colour combinations. Try different textures and modify anything and everything to suit your taste.

I don't want to be called a crafting dictator, but when you read this book there are a few rules that you simply must follow. Firstly, you must allow yourself to completely enjoy the process of crafting and leave behind the whining children, the dishes and the cat's meows. Put on some slippers, some great music and relax. I'd suggest a glass of wine, but I know one friend who sewed right over her thumb after a

quick drink, so better not. You need to be able to concentrate whilst you enjoy yourself!

Second, you must give up being a perfectionist. If you approach craft (or anything) as a perfectionist you can kill it so easily. Your little inner crafting child needs encouragement at this point, not criticism. So, put perfectionism behind and coax your imagination to come out to play. Now, gather together the materials, set aside an hour of time and follow the easy instructions to produce your masterpiece.

Enjoy! *Maria Binns*

Sewing

Appliqué Name Cushion

These are so pretty! They make lovely gifts for a baby's birth, children's beds or for yourself. Why remake the cushion cover when someone else has done a fine job? There is no point. It is better to spend your time embellishing a pre-made cushion cover. These are inexpensive to buy. Experiment with using block letters, or other letters. Different lettering can be found in abundance on the internet!

MATERIALS

- Cream coloured pre-made cotton cushion cover (available at all furniture stores or department stores)

- Cushion

- Fabrics in assorted colours and patterns – a different fabric for each letter

- White paper

- Beige coloured cotton thread

- Dishcloth

- Scissors

- Letters

- Double-sided iron-on appliqué paper

INSTRUCTIONS

Print out from your computer and trace the letters onto white paper. Cut them out **(1)**.

Pin the letters to chosen fabrics and cut out a square of fabric around each letter **(2)**.

Cut out the same sized squares of appliqué paper for each letter in the name. **(3)**

Take the pins out for step 4. Place the dish cloth onto the ironing board, followed by the fabric facing down with the appliqué paper on the top (leave the protective layer on the back of the appliqué paper).

Iron with a hot iron to stick the fabric to the appliqué paper. **(4)** This is a very neat little trick that will save your iron from being ruined by the glue. Repeat this for all the letters.

Pin the paper letters to the fabric squares again and cut them out neatly. **(5)**

1

2

3

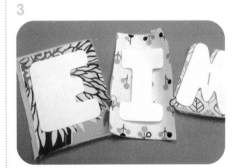

4

5

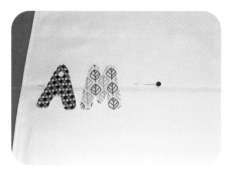

6

7

8

Fold the cushion cover in half from the top, open it out and place a line of pins across the mid-line. Start to pin the fabric letters onto the cushion with their centres on the mid-line you have marked **(6)**.

When you have placed all the letters, carefully remove all the pins. Check that the letters are evenly spaced on the cushion cover. **(7)**

Take the backing paper off the letters and iron them to the cushion cover. Open the zip at the bottom. **(8)**

Thread your machine, and put it onto the zigzag stitch. Adjust the stitch width to the narrowest setting. Sew around the edge of each letter slowly, placing the cushion opening over the arm of the sewing machine.

This will be the most time consuming part of this project. **(9)**

9

When you are finished, place the cushion inside the cover.

The Sweet Suzy Bag

When sewing you will do well to make your sewing machine, iron, spray water gun and pins your very best friends. Out of these, I think that my iron is my very, very best friend when sewing and chasing accuracy. Remember that accuracy saves you time and means that you will not go over your time limit by unpicking mistakes. A little bit of care goes a long way.

MATERIALS

- 4 main pattern pieces: 1 in main fabric, 1 in complementary fabric 2 in iron-on interfacing

- 2 strap pieces: 1 in complementary fabric and 1 in iron-on interfacing

- 2 flap pieces: 1 in complementary fabric and 1 in iron-on interfacing

- 1 button covered in main material

- 1 magnet closure

INSTRUCTIONS

The seam allowances have been included. For this little bag, be clever with stripes; a combination of a striped and a patterned material looks great. I also like the contrast of a small bag which uses a material with a large-ish pattern. **(1)** Lay the pattern onto your chosen pieces of fabric. Cut out the main 2 pattern pieces, 1 in the main fabric pattern and the other in the complementary fabric.

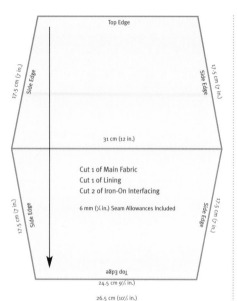

Top Edge

17.5 cm (7 in.) Side Edge

Side Edge

17.5 cm (7 in.) Side Edge

31 cm (12 in.)

Cut 1 of Main Fabric
Cut 1 of Lining
Cut 2 of Iron-On Interfacing

6 mm (¼ in.) Seam Allowances Included

17.5 cm (7 in.) Side Edge

Side Edge 17.5 cm (7 in.)

Top Edge

24.5 cm 9½ in.)

26.5 cm (10½ in.)

Magnet Clasp

13.5 cm (5 in.) Side Edge

Bag Flap Piece

Side Edge

Fold

Cut 1 of Complementary Fabric
Cut 1 of Iron-on Interfacing

13.5 cm (5 in.) Side Edge

Side Edge

Cut here

26.5 cm (10½ in.)

1

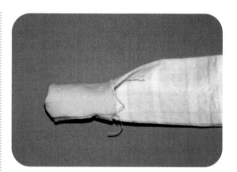

2

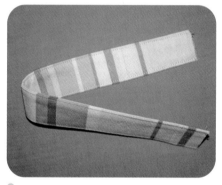

3

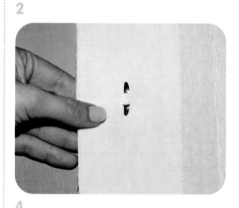

4

Measure and cut the main bag piece. Measure and cut the main bag piece from your contrasting fabric. Use fun contrasting colours. Measure and cut the flap piece from your contrasting fabric. Cut out the iron-on interfacing from all the pieces and iron them on.

Measure and cut a piece of the complimentary fabric for straps 35cm/13in. long and 9cm/3.5in.

wide. Pin and sew the two long edges together, right sides facing each other. Turn the strap the right way out and iron it flat. **(2)**

Finish the strap with two lines of top stitching along each edge – as close to the edge as possible. **(3)**

Fold the flap piece in half lengthwise. Attach the 'outie' part of the magnet

of the metal button piece and press down the button back. Hand sew the button onto the front of the bag flap, opposite side to the 'outie' magnetic clasp. **(5, 6, & 7)**

Fold the main bag piece in half, right sides facing. Sew down both sides from the top opening to the bottom fold of the bag, leaving a 6mm/¼in. seam allowance. **(8)** Attach the 'innie' magnet clasp to the main bag piece 5cm/2in. from the top opening.

Take the main bag piece and open the top. Press down the bottom corners into points. **(9)**. Pin these and sew a straight line across about 3cm/1 ⅛in. from the point. This will give the bag a square bottom. **(10, 11)**

Sew the bag lining in the same way as you sewed the main bag piece, leaving a 5cm/2in. hole in one side seam. You will need this to pull the bag to the right side when it is finished.

clasp to the flap piece, 3.5cm/1½in. from the middle fold. **(4)** Fold the flap in half, right sides facing. Sew a seam down each side leaving a 6mm/¼in. seam allowance. Turn the flap inside out and iron it flat.

Cut out a circle of complimentary fabric for your covered button. Fold the edges of the fabric into the centre

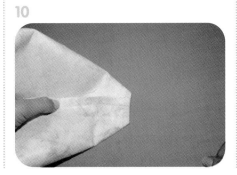

12

13

14

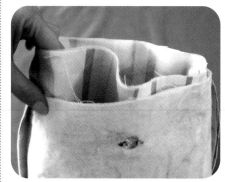

15

16

Pin the flap onto top edge of the main bag piece, right sides together. Pin the strap onto either side of the bag, right sides facing also. Sew around the top of the bag with a row (or two) of straight stitching, attaching both the straps and flap to the main bag piece. **(12, 13)**.

Turn the main bag piece inside out, tucking the flap and strap inside. **(14)**

Put the lining piece inside the main bag piece, right sides facing. **(15)** Pin the top edges of the main bag and lining together. Sew around the top edge, joining the lining and main bag piece.

Pull the bag right side out, through the hole you left in one side of the lining. Hand-sew the hole in the lining shut. Top stitch around the top opening of the bag.

Tuck the lining into the main piece of the bag and pull out the straps and flap. Iron the bag to give it a lovely shape. Ironing the bag with a book inside it will give it a great shape. **(16)** You can use starch if you want to make it stiffer. This looks great! **(17)**

Humbug Bean Bag

I love this shape. After I designed the humbug party bags (see page 48), I turned to the sewing chapter of this book and began designing a bean bag. I was really wondering how to make a bean bag in an hour, when I thought about the humbug design. I then met up with my twin sister, Emma (a brilliant seamstress), brainstormed and came up with this great design.

This pattern is funky, comfy and the easiest beanbag pattern I have ever come across. I hope you love it as much as we do! If you want to make a quick prototype of the shape, try making the party bag before you make this bean bag.

MATERIALS

- 2m/6ft 6in. Cotton fabric (furniture fabric works well). The fabric needs to be at least 1m/3ft 3in. wide.

- 1m/3ft 3in continuous zipper

- Cotton thread

- Scissors

- Ruler

- Pins

- Bag of styrofoam balls

- Zipper foot for sewing machine

INSTRUCTIONS

Measure and cut out a large piece of fabric 1m/3ft 3in x 2m/6ft 6in. **(1)**

Fold the piece of material in half, with the right sides facing. Pin the two edges opposite the fold together. **(2)**

Sew this seam together using a straight stitch and leaving a 1.7cm/⅝ in. seam allowance. Iron the seam open and pin the zipper along the middle of the seam upside down. **(3)**

Place a zipper foot in your sewing machine. Start at one end and sew, using a straight stitch along the zipper from one end to the other. Sew as close to the zipper as you can.

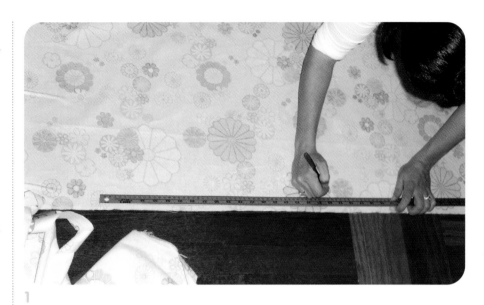

1

When you reach the end, sew across the end and down the other side in the same way. When you reach the end of the zipper, pivot the needle and sew back and forth a few times

across the end. Turn the material right side out to check that you have inserted your zipper correctly. **(4)** Lay the bean bag flat and it will be a

2

3

4

square shape. You should still have the bean bag inside out at this point. With one side folded with no seam, and the side opposite with a zipper in it, choose one of the two open sides and sew a seam along it, leaving a 1.7cm/⅝in. seam allowance. Zigzag along the edges to prevent fraying.

Now the bean bag is becoming a humbug shape. Laid on the ground, your bag now looks like a pocket with three sides joined and one left open. Take this opening and close it, with the zipper and the fold meeting in the middle. This will make your humbug shape. Pin and sew this seam with a straight stitch, leaving a seam allowance of 1.7cm/⅝in. **(5)**. Zigzag the edge. Open the seam on top of the zipper with a stitch ripper **(6)**.

Open up the zipper and turn the bean bag the right way out. Fill it with styrofoam balls and close the zipper. **(7)**

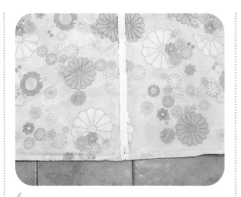

6

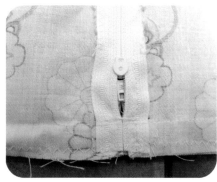

5

7

Torn Fabric Basket

MATERIALS

- Cotton cord piping

- Assorted pile of material (100% cotton) scraps (old sheets also work wonderfully)

- Neutral coloured thread

- Sewing machine

- Scissors

- Measuring tape

- A few clothes pegs

I love these baskets that are so clever and quick to sew. They are a little fiddly at first but it is amazing to see your basket take shape as you sew. The basket will be wider and shallower if you use thicker material. Using thin cotton and winding it tightly around the cord will ensure a deeper, smaller basket.

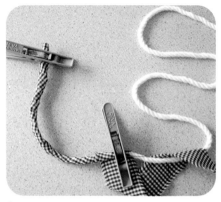

INSTRUCTIONS

Rip about ten 2.5cm/1in. strips of assorted material scraps. This is just to start with – you may need to rip more. Rip fabric by making a small cut into it then ripping from selvage to selvage. Children love helping with this. Take one end of the cord and begin to wrap a strip of fabric around it. **(1)**

Secure the end with a clothes peg while you wrap this first part. **(2)**

As you do this, start to coil the cord. The beginning is the trickiest. **(3)**

When you have coiled the cord three times, using the zigzag stitch on your sewing machine, start to sew the cord together in a coil.

The ditch between the two pieces of cord needs to be in the middle of the stitch so that both pieces of cord are

caught in the stitch. Sew slowly. Continue wrapping the material around the cord. When you have wrapped about 10cm/4in., place a peg to hold it and continue to zigzag the coil together. **(4)**

When there is about 2.5cm/1 in. of material strip left, take another strip in a different fabric and start wrapping it over the coil. The two strips will overlap for about an inch which will hold it in place. **(5)**

Continue wrapping, then sewing the coil together. **(6)**

As you sew the coils together, it automatically winds up into a basket shape. **(7)**

When you reach the end of the cord, zigzag to the end. You may need to go over it again to make it secure. **(8)**

6

7

8

Velvet Bow Clips

These are so sweet! I have made loads and loads of these little babies. If you want a more edgy look, go for black velvet. These look great in long hair at the top of a pony tail or in short hair to sweep back a fringe.

MATERIALS

- 1 metal barrette clip.
- 40cm/16in. velvet ribbon
- Needle and thread
- Tailors chalk
- Pinking shears
- Scissors
- Hot glue gun

INSTRUCTIONS

Cut a 40cm/16in. length of velvet ribbon and pink the edges to prevent fraying. Draw a line to mark the middle of the ribbon. Mark two more lines 10cm/4in. from each end. **(1)**

Start with one ribbon end. With the velvet side of the ribbon facing the table, fold the first line to meet the middle line. Hold this loop between your fingers. Insert a pin through the layers to hold it in place. **(2)**

Take the remainder of the ribbon and loop it over into the middle of the ribbon, so that now there are two loops at this end, and pin in place. Thread your needle and sew through all the ribbon layers 2.5cm/1in. from

1

2

3

4

5

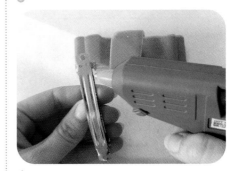

6

7

the centre. **(3)** Repeat steps 3–5 for the remaining side of ribbon.

Place the bow onto the barrette and measure another piece of ribbon to fit around the middle with an overlap. Cut this piece. **(4)**

Using your needle and thread, sew this piece around the bow at the back. **(5)**

Hot glue the back of the bow onto the barrette. **(6)**

Hold the bow firmly in place for approximately one minute until the glue dries. **(7)**

Tsunami Kanzashi

When I first discovered these little Japanese fabric flowers, I was in heaven. They are like origami, made with fabric. There are so many uses for them. You can sew them to teddy bears or soft toys, handbags, shoes or barrettes.

These look like they would be so fiddly to make but they are not at all. They are very straightforward – and fun!

MATERIALS

- Cotton fabric – I have found that thick cottons work very well

- Spray-on starch

- Clothes pegs

- Cotton thread

- Needle

- Scissors

- Ruler

- Rotary cutter (or use scissors)

- Cutting board

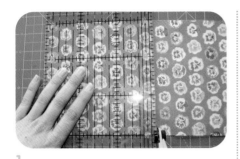

1

2

3

4

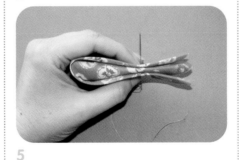

5

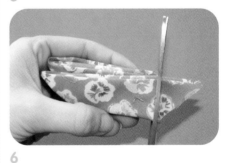

6

INSTRUCTIONS

Before I use the fabric, I usually spray it with starch and iron it so that it keeps its shape better when it is in a petal shape.

Using your rotary cutter, ruler and cutting board, cut eight squares of the same fabric, 6.5cm/2.5in. x 6.5cm/2.5in. **(1)**

To start folding, place a fabric square on the table in front of you with one point towards you, right side down. Fold the square into the triangle with the point facing you. **(2)**

Fold the two side points of the triangle into the middle point, the one facing you. Now you have a gap in the middle of the square you have folded. **(3)**

Fold the square in half. You will now have a triangle shape with a gap in

the middle. Pinch the open end between your fingers. Turn the fabric over and fold the two corners into the centre. **(4)**

Thread a needle and tie a knot in the end. Sew through the end you are pinching with a tacking stitch. Make a knot. **(5)**

Cut away the pointy end of the petal. **(6)** Don't cut through the tacking stitch.

7

8

9

Repeat steps 3–7 to make all eight petals for your flower. **(7)**

Thread a needle with a double thread. Sew through each petal at the end, joining them in a line. **(8)**

Sew through the first petal again and pull the thread taught to make a flower shape. Fasten your thread with a knot. **(9)**

Shape the petals, by pressing down on the tops to round them out. **(10)**

Sew a button (covered buttons look great also) into the middle to cover the rough ends and form the centre of the flower.

10

Fabric Button Hair Ties

This is a very quick project. I love little things you can make to quench your creative thirst and still produce something really useful and pretty. I have made a pile of these for my daughter who wears them to school every day. If you have short hair, make the bobby pin version for a very cute touch. With more time you could even embroider a little picture or name onto the fabric to make the hair tie more personalised.

MATERIALS

• Stunning fabric scraps (Japanese kimono fabrics look amazing for this)

• Button covering gadget (bought at fabric stores)

• Metal button and back in the size you prefer – I used a large button for this tutorial

• Scissors

• Pencil

• Hair elastic

INSTRUCTIONS

Place the metal button onto your fabric and trace a ring around it, leaving a 1cm/⅝in. seam allowance. **(1)**

Cut around this line. Your cutting does not have to be perfect as you won't see this part. **(2)**

Place your fabric circle into the round rubber indent. Press the metal button on top of this. Fold in all the edges, catching them on the teeth of the metal button. **(3)**

Place the button back on top and press down with the plastic piece. **(4)**

Remove the button from the machine and you should have a perfect covered button. **(5)**

Take a hair elastic and put it through the loop on the back of the button. Pull the hair band back over the loop and through itself to secure. **(6)**

Tie the button into your hair.

1

2

3

4

5

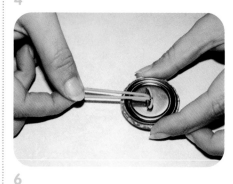

6

Picnic Rug Bag

(also nicknamed the Brug)

My lovely twin sister Emma designed this very clever picnic rug that folds into a bag. I fell in love. In good design, form follows function, and this definitely adheres to that golden rule. What could be more functional than a gorgeous tote bag (filled with your sunglasses, a book and your sunscreen to carry on a day out), which then folds out to a soft rug when you arrive at your park or beach? And I am quite taken with the nickname I came up with.

If you cannot find a fleece rug to buy, cut your own and make sure that the bag piece is a rectangular piece one third as wide as your rug and one third as long.

MATERIALS

- Fleece rug 90cm/36in. x 70cm/28in.

- 2 other pieces of sturdy fabric 33cm/14in. x 26.5cm/10in.

- 80cm/32 in. cotton canvas strapping

- Cotton thread in a neutral shade

- Scissors

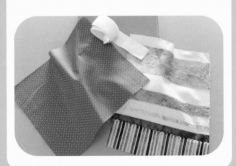

1

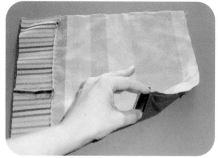

2

3

4

5

6

INSTRUCTIONS

Cut out the two pieces of bag material, both the same size. Pin them together with the right sides facing. **(1)**

Leave a 1.7cm/⅝in. seam allowance and sew the two pieces of fabric together with a straight stitch, leaving a 5cm/2in. gap in the side. **(2)**

Sew around the edges with a zigzag stitch to reinforce, still leaving the gap in one side. **(3)**

Take your strap material, fold both ends in half and sew together. **(4)**

Pin each end of the strap to the corners of the inside of the bag and secure by sewing in a square shape with a straight stitch. **(5)**

Turn the bag right way out, through the hole left in the side. The right side of the fabric should be facing out now. It should look like this. **(6)**

Measure and mark the midpoint of the bag. **(7)**

7

8

9

Measure and mark the midpoint of the bottom edge of the rug. Pin the bag, right side facing down, onto the bottom of the rug with both midpoints matched. Face the top of the bag towards the middle of the rug. **(8)**

Sew the bag to the rug with a straight stitch and a very tiny seam allowance. Sew up three sides only, leaving the top of the bag (where the straps are attached) open. **(9)**

Fold the rug into this middle part, then turn it inside out. This is so clever. Your rug has now folded into a bag. **(10)**

10

The Most Useful Tote Bag

I can't stand shopping with ugly environmentally friendly bags, so this is my answer to eco-friendly shopping. I have organised sewing nights at my house where friends bring chocolate, paté and their sewing machines, just to try out a new pattern I have designed. And this got the thumbs up! Most people made three bags in about two hours. Those who used overlockers easily sewed up a tote in twenty-five minutes. I have made a lot of these as presents for people who have helped with childcare and with my website. I have also swapped some of these bags over the internet. Why not organise a sewing night at your house or your own tote swap?

MATERIALS

- 1m/3ft. cotton fabric
- 1m/3ft. contrasting cotton fabric for lining
- Cotton thread
- Scissors
- Sewing machine or overlocker

INSTRUCTIONS

Measure and cut two pieces of fabric 35cm/14in. wide and 45cm/18in. long from your main fabric. Measure and cut two pieces the same size from the contrasting fabric. Two bright colours look great together.

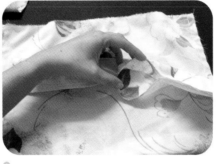

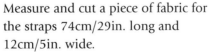

Measure and cut a piece of fabric for the straps 74cm/29in. long and 12cm/5in. wide.

Zigzag around all the edges to prevent fraying. Using an overlocker to sew will mean you can skip this step. **(1)**

Pin the main pattern pieces together with the right sides facing. Sew both edges and the bottom together, using a straight stitch, leaving a 1cm/⅝in. seam allowance. **(2)**

Sew together the two lining pieces, but leave a 10cm/4in. hole in the bottom seam. **(3)**

Fold the strap piece in half, with right sides facing. Iron, then sew or overlock this long seam together, leaving a small seam allowance. **(4)**

Cut the strap in half to make two straps. Turn each strap right side out and iron them, with the seam on the side of the strap. Top stitch down both edges of each strap. **(5)**

5

6

Pin the strap pieces to the outer edge of the main bag piece. Sew them on with a straight stitch. Reinforce by sewing this line a few times and backstitching. **(6)**

Take the main bag piece and turn it inside out, tucking the straps into the middle. **(7)**

7

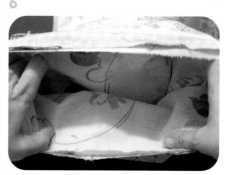

8

Now hold the lining, right sides out, and place it inside the main bag piece. Pin the top edges together and sew around the top edge, leaving a 1cm/⅝in. seam allowance. **(8, 9)**

Turn the bag the right way out by gently pulling it through the hole in the bottom seam of the lining. And finally, sew a line of stitch to close the hole in the bottom of the lining. **(10)**

9

10

Iron the bag so that it sits well and top stitch around the top of it.

Felt

Machine Felting

There are so many things you can do with wool, apart from the obvious, knitting. When I discovered machine felting a few years ago, I thought it was the best thing since sliced bread. In fact I still do! It is so simple and easy to do. Felting mats all the knitted stitches together into one piece of fabric. This means that, after being felted, you can use this felt just as if it were a piece of fabric. You can cut into it without it fraying and sew it, both by hand or using a machine. Dye it, embroider it, glue it. The options are unlimited.

The first step before you begin to felt is a trip to a thrift store or to your grandma's house. Find an old woollen jumper. I have found that the best pullovers to use are those really gaudy numbers with geometrical shapes. They produce awesome bags. Or cream cable pullovers with floral patterns look great made into felted flower cushions or bears.

MATERIALS

- One or two pure wool pullovers (make sure that they are 100% wool as acrylic does not felt).

- Three pairs of jeans or rough fabric

- Normal washing powder

- A washing machine

INSTRUCTIONS

Set the washing machine to hot, with a cold rinse. (Yes, at this point you may realise that you have inadvertently felted many articles before. You know when your jumper came out of the wash four sizes too small? That was felting. What a pity you threw it out!)

Place the jumpers into the washing machine along with something that will cause friction. I have had a lot of success with a few pairs of tough jeans.

Put the washing powder into the machine and turn it on. I always choose the longest cycle.

When the washing cycle is finished, check to see how the jumpers are doing, and put them in again. You will need to wash them between four and six times to achieve the desired effect.

When you pull the jumpers out of the machine and they have shrunk significantly and all the stitches appear joined so tightly you can barely distinguish them from each other, you are done.

Now you are ready to take this felt and do some incredible things with it. There is nothing like crafting while lying in front of the TV doing very little is there?

Felted Cushion

This is a great way to make old pullovers into fantastic one-off cushions. A pile of different felted cushions on the couch looks amazing. These are so easy and surprising, they are in fact a little addictive to make. I have been known to try to whisk away pullovers from family members, way before they want to hand them over, just because I am sure they would make stunning cushions! Before you start, read the Machine Felting tutorial and felt an old pullover to use.

MATERIALS

- A felted woollen pullover

- A cushion which fits comfortably inside your felted pullover

- A ball of yarn

- 3 buttons

- Cotton thread

- A large needle

- Scissors

INSTRUCTIONS

Lay your felted pullover down on a table and carefully cut off both sleeves at the seams. **(1)**

Cut along the top seam of the jumper from each sleeve to the neck. **(2)**

Place the cushion inside the pullover and push it down to the bottom to make sure of the fit. Remove the cushion, turn the pullover inside out and sew the bottom together with a straight stitch on your sewing machine. **(3)**

Turn the pullover right side out again and push the cushion back inside, right down to the bottom. On each side of the pullover mark the point to which the cushion reaches with two pins. Remove the cushion, turn the pullover inside out and machine sew the side seams to these points. **(4)**

Turn the pullover right side out again, placing the cushion inside. Cut the neck from the front of the pullover, leaving enough felt to be able to tuck this front flap behind the cushion. **(5)**.

1

2

3

4

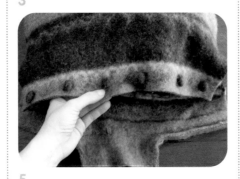

5

6

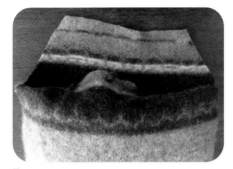

7

8

9

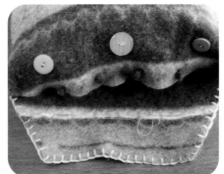

10

Cut the bottom flap into an envelope shape, cutting off the corners and the neck ribbing. **(6)**

Tuck the front flap of the cushion cover behind the cushion. **(7)**

Take a large needle and a long piece of yarn and starting at one side blanket stitch around the entire edge of the envelope-shaped flap. End with a secure knot. **(8)**

Hold the flap over the cushion and mark the buttonholes with pins or tailor's chalk. Lift the flap up and make the corresponding marks on the layer underneath. **(9)**

Sew the buttons onto the cushion at the marked points. **(10)**

11

Cut button holes at the marked points. Make the holes smaller than your button as felt has a lot of give and take. Do up the buttons and you now have your lovely cushion. **(11)**

Felted Lavender Sleep Bear

This bear has helped me get to sleep on many nights. It is a variation of a herbal sleep pillow and another great use for a felted pullover. This little bear can be constructed in less than half an hour. If you want it to be a tiny bear for a child, why not shrink the pattern on a photocopier and make a tiny bear. Use your imagination and add eyes, a nose, rickrack. The sky is the limit.

MATERIALS

- Bear pattern piece
- Felted wool
- A ball of yarn
- Large needle
- Dried lavender
- Teaspoon

1

2

3

METHOD

Thread a large needle with a very long piece of wool. Double it over and tie together with a double knot. **(1)**

Using the pattern, cut out your two bear pieces in felt. Now sew the eyes on the front piece of felt. Sew one stitch and then another in a cross over it. **(2)**

Sew the next eye on the front piece in the same way, tie a knot at the back and cut off the excess yarn. **(3)**

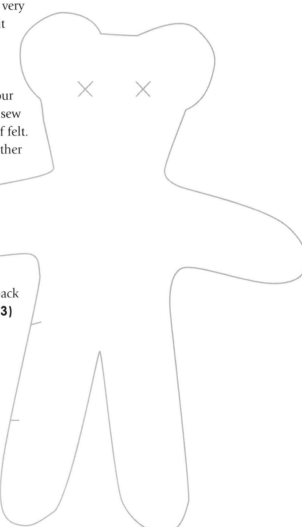

4

5

6

7

8

Begin sewing around the bear on the left thigh. Place the two bear pieces together, right side out. Tie a knot at the end of the yarn and sew through the top of the bear from underneath. **(4)**

Now sew through the two layers and continue sewing the two pieces together with a simple straight stitch. **(5, 6)**

When you have sewn around most of the bear, leave a 5cm/2in. gap to put the lavender into. **(7)**

Spoon 6–8 teaspoons of dried lavender into the bear's belly and head. **(8)**

Sew the gap up and tie a secure knot in your yarn at the back of the bear.

Paper

Tulip Doily Lights

Humbug Party Bags

Ribbon Card

Christmas Ribbon Card

Star Garland

Tulip Doily Lights

These ethereal little shades can be used to spruce up an old lamp, like I have done, or a string of fairy lights. When the lights are turned on, they throw delicate, lacy patterns onto the walls. They are a great way to bring romance to your house.

MATERIALS

- White paper doilies, rectangular, square or circle shaped
- Sticky dots
- PVA glue
- Small paintbrush
- Scissors

INSTRUCTIONS

Cut the doily into a square by folding it into a triangle, and cutting any excess away. Leave the doily folded in a triangle, with the point facing away from you. **(1)**

1

2

3

4

5

6

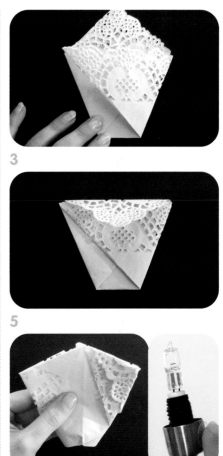

7

8

Fold the left corner of the triangle to right side of the larger triangle. **(2)**

Fold the right corner of the triangle to the left side, crossing over the first fold. **(3)**

Unfold these sides and glue them back in the same way. **(4)**

Fold down the top point of paper to make a flap on the front. Flip the tulip over and fold down the point on the other side. **(5)**

Cut a small hole in the bottom of the tulip. The hole needs to be big enough to fit over the fairy light and onto the base. **(6)**

Hold the tulip in your hand and fold it in half, so that there are now four creases in the light shade. **(7)**

Place two sticky dots on the base of the fairy light. **(8)**

Slide the tulip onto the fairy light and press it firmly onto the sticky dots.

Repeat all the steps above until you have covered all the fairy lights with paper shades.

Humbug Party Bags

I love these little bags! They have a myriad of uses. Use bright colours and fill with stickers and candy for children's party bags. Delicate papers in muted colours, filled with sugared almonds make perfect wedding treats.

MATERIALS

• 2 paper squares 20cm/8in. x 20cm/8in.

• Small piece of ribbon

• Thread

• Candy/treats to put inside the bags

1

2

3

INSTRUCTIONS

Place the sheets of paper together, wrong sides together. (**1**)

Sew together one side of the square with a straight stitch, leaving a 1cm/⅜in. seam allowance. (**2**)

Pivot the paper and continue sewing the next side together. When you are near the corner fold the ribbon in half to make a loop, tuck it in between the two sheets and sew over it. (**3**)

Pivot the paper again and sew the third side together to make a pocket. (**4**)

Place the candy or treats inside the pocket. Make sure not to overstuff it. (**5**)

4

5

6

Remove the bag from the sewing machine. Take the bag, open up the remaining side to make the humbug shape, place the two seams on top of each other, and fold a seam over

7

to close the bag. (**6**)

Sew the last side together. This side may be a little more tricky to sew because of the bulk. (**7**)

Ribbon Card

If you leave your sewing machine threaded, a little card like this will take you about five minutes, if not, six. On a lot of occasions I have sewn one of these cards on the way out the door to a party, in between applying lipgloss and mascara. They are honestly quicker to make than driving to the shops, getting out of the car and walking inside. Sometimes I will spend an hour and make loads of them. I store them in a gorgeous box, to be used when needed.

MATERIALS

- Pre-cut blank cards
- Ribbon, lace, wool, fabric scraps, feathers, etc.
- 3 or 4 buttons
- PVA glue
- Paint brush
- Glue gun
- Thread
- Sewing machine

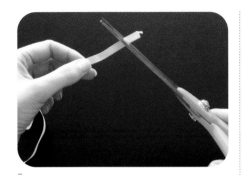
1

2

3

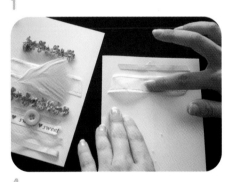
4

5

6

INSTRUCTIONS

Cut small pieces of ribbon, wool and lace to fit across the card horizontally. **(1)**

Arrange them in a line going down the card. Experiment with different colours and textures. **(2)**

Place the ribbons and lace on the table in the same arrangement and paint a small line of glue down the middle of your card. **(3)**

Stick the fabric, lace and ribbons onto the card. **(4)**

Sew a straight line on top of the glue, down the centre of card. Sew other lines if you wish. **(5)**

Heat up your hot glue gun and carefully glue buttons onto the card, on top of the stitching and scraps. **(6)**

Christmas Ribbon Card

MATERIALS

- Pre-cut black or coloured card

- Green ribbons (different shades and widths)

- Adhesive plastic (the kind used to cover books)

- Scissors

- Buttons

- Glue stick

- Glue gun

- Thread

- Sewing machine

These cards are yet another variation of the ribbon card. Really, the possibilities for card like this are limitless.

INSTRUCTIONS

Cut out a piece of adhesive paper just smaller than the front of your card. **(1)**

Peel the backing paper from the adhesive plastic and lay it on the table, sticky side facing up. **(2)**

Cut lengths of ribbon the same width as the plastic and stick them to it, leaving small gaps between them. **(3)**

Cut both sides of the plastic, to make a triangular, tree shape. **(4)**

Carefully lift the ribbon pieces one by one from the plastic and glue to the card in the same pattern. **(5)**

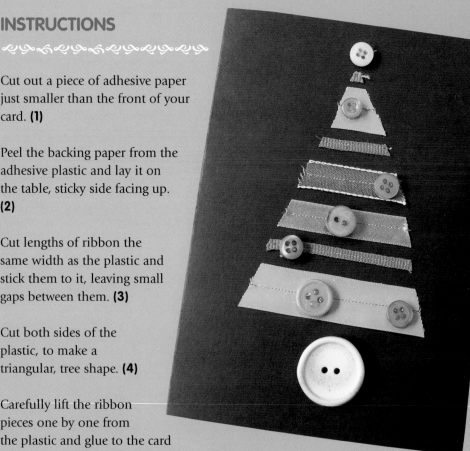

1

2

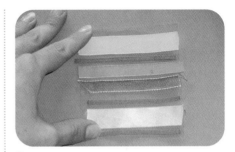

3

4

5

6

7

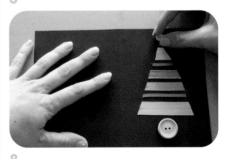

8

Sew with a straight stitch. You can either sew down the centre of each ribbon or sew along the edges of the triangle and through the middle. **(6)**

Cut the loose ends. **(7)**

Using your hot glue gun, glue a large button at the base of the tree and a smaller button at the top of it. **(8)**

Glue some colourful smaller buttons onto the tree to look like Christmas baubles.

Fold your card in half and write in the centre. You can buy white paint pens to write on black or coloured card.

Star Garland

This garland is very easy to construct and people will be stumped as to how you made it. The sewing is very simple and appropriate even for complete beginners. Be sure to use a very strong needle in your machine when sewing paper. Use silver paper for a minimalist look or brightly coloured papers for a bolder touch to Christmas. Garlands hung straight down in a window or a doorway look incredible.

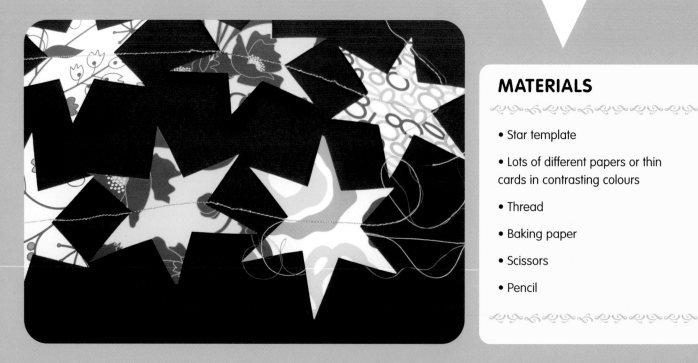

MATERIALS

- Star template
- Lots of different papers or thin cards in contrasting colours
- Thread
- Baking paper
- Scissors
- Pencil

1

2

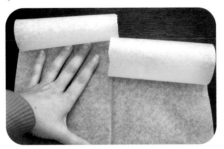

3

4

INSTRUCTIONS

Trace the star template onto your paper or card with a pencil. **(1)**

Carefully cut out about twenty stars. If you want a garland to wrap around a Christmas tree, cut about forty. **(2)**

Tear off a piece of baking paper 30cm/1ft long and tear it in half to save paper. **(3)**

Start at one end of the baking paper and sew a 15cm/6in. line of straight stitch down the centre. **(4)**

Place a star onto the middle of the baking paper and sew over it, through the centre. **(5)**

5

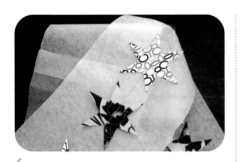

6

7

8

Continue sewing the baking paper for about 15cm/6in. and then sew on another star. Repeat this to sew all the stars onto the baking paper. **(6)**

When you are near the end of the piece of baking paper, tuck another piece under the first and continue sewing. **(7)**

When you have sewn all stars onto the paper, hold the paper in your hands and carefully rip the baking paper away from each star until you are left with your garland. **(8)**

Drape your garland around your Christmas tree or hang in billows above a fireplace. **(9)**

9

Clay

Using Paper Clay

I love paper clay. It is just clay with paper added to it. Paper clay is readily available and is bought in a slab at a pottery store. It is very inexpensive. The paper means that it is easier to work with for the beginner, and it can be wetted again when it is dry. Also it is much less likely to explode when being fired. You can produce great clay in under an hour.

In this book I have not factored in firing time for your clay. That would push this clay into a very time-consuming craft. But as you don't have to do anything when it is being fired, there is no point including it. Your first firing may take about eight hours, while the second firing after you have glazed may take about ten. It is easy to get clay fired at pottery stores or at a local potter's guild. It costs next to nothing. In fact, I am sure you will be pleasantly surprised at how inexpensive it is to make these things.

Clay is messy. Wear an apron, and if you can work outside or in the garage, it is a great idea. If I work at home, I just use the kitchen bench and wear really old clothes and an apron.

In this tutorial I will be teaching basic techniques for working with paper clay, which you will use over and over again.

MATERIALS

- 1 block paper clay x 2
- 30cm/1ft fishing line or Tigertail
- 2 pegs
- Rolling pin
- Lace scraps, rickrack, fern, leaves, etc.
- Glaze – bought at a pottery store
- Big paintbrush

Methods to use before you begin working with your clay.

1. Cutting

Make an easy tool to cut the clay by tying a 30cm/1ft length of fishing line onto two pegs. To cut the clay, hold a peg in each hand, pull the line taught and push it into the clay, easily separating it. **(1)**

When you have a large chunk to cut into a smaller chunk, place the line underneath the big chunk and holding the pegs pull it through the clay, cutting it in half. **(2)**

1

2

2. Wedging

Take the chunk of clay you have cut and place it onto a bench. With the bottom of your palms, press one end of the clay into the table. Turn the clay over and repeat this process over and over for about three minutes. **(1)** If you are wedging correctly the clay will look like a bull's head. **(2)** This step is necessary to soften the clay so it is workable and to make sure that you get all the air bubbles. If left in the clay, air bubbles can cause it to explode in the kiln. **(3)**

1

2

3

3. Rolling

Use a wooden rolling pin to roll the clay out onto the bench. Roll the pin quickly over the clay, using moderate pressure. Roll the pin in all directions. If you see lumps in the clay, there are air bubbles and you will have to wedge it again to get them out.

1

For making the vase in this book, roll the clay out to the same thickness as your thumb. For the ornaments, roll the clay out to about half the thickness of your thumb. **(1)**

4. Print Rolling

Print rolling your clay is literally pressing prints into it with your rolling pin. This technique creates amazing textures in the clay. To print roll, take a piece of clay which has already been wedged and rolled out. Place a leaf, lace, rick rack or feathers onto the clay slab and using your rolling pin, roll the print into the clay. **(1)** Then lift the leaf (or other medium) from the clay and you are left with an imprint. **(2)**

1

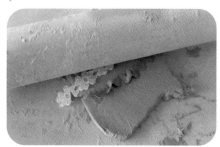

2

Methods to use after you have constructed your clay object

1. Drying

It is very important that your paper clay object is completely dry before you fire it. If not, it will explode in the kiln. The drying process takes a few days. If you are in a real hurry for the clay to dry, with paper clay you can cheat a bit and dry it with a hairdryer for about 20 minutes on a medium heat. But I recommend waiting for it to air dry. When the clay is dry, it has no moisture left in. It feels hard and brittle to touch and is white.

2. First Firing

I recommend taking your clay to your local pottery shop to have it fired. It is very inexpensive and no fuss at all! Paper clay is fired at 1000°C/1832°F. If you are firing it yourself, you will need to learn about your kiln and work out how long it will take your kiln to work up to this temperature. An automatic kiln will switch off when it reaches this temperature and the piece will be fired.

After the first firing your piece will be hard and ready to be glazed.

3. Glazing

Glazing is just like painting. Use the biggest brush you can and paint on your glaze. Read the instructions on the jar for the particular glaze you are using.

When you are buying your glaze, make sure that it is suitable for paper clay.

For pots and vases, don't glaze the bottom of the vessel. This will make it stick to the bottom of the kiln.

4. Second Firing

Now that you have glazed the clay, you need to fire it again to make the glaze come to life. Once again, I recommend taking the piece to your local pottery store and having it fired. For the second firing, paper clay is fired at 1080°C/1976°F

After the second firing you will be able to see and hold your masterpiece. It is the most amazing transformation from a piece of earth into a gorgeous vessel.

Paper Clay Ornaments and Mobile

These little ornaments look fantastic on a Christmas tree or you can string them on twine and hang them as a mobile. I have not glazed these little ornaments, but have used another technique to paint them. Because I have painted the ornaments, I have only fired them once to strengthen the clay.

Print rolling and stamping the clay is addictive when you see how amazing these techniques look in the final product.

MATERIALS

- Paper clay
- Cookie cutters
- Rolling pin
- Skewer
- Stamps

INSTRUCTIONS

Note: Before you begin this tutorial read the Using Paper Clay tutorial (pages 58–60) and follow the instructions for cutting, wedging and rolling the clay.

Roll your clay out to half or ⅔ the thickness of your thumb. **(1)**

Make patterns in the clay by imprinting it. Place lace or rickrack onto the clay, then roll over the top of it with your rolling pin. Pull away the lace and the clay is left with a gorgeous imprint. **(2)**

To texturise the clay, you could also use stamps. Take a stamp and press it into the clay. These look fantastic! **(3)**

Press the cookie cutters into the clay. **(4)**

Lift up the cookie cutters and gently pull away the excess clay from the clay pieces. **(5)**

Press a skewer into the clay piece to make a hole in it. **(6)**

Now you have finished constructing your ornaments, leave them to dry for a few days and then have them fired (read the instructions in the Using Paper Clay tutorial). **(7)**

When the ornaments have been fired, paint them with a thin coat of acrylic paint. Take a wet cloth and wipe off most of the paint, leaving it mainly in the grooves of the patterns and imprints. **(8)**

Thread leather or twine throug the hole in your ornament so it can be hung up. **(9)**

To make a mobile
When you have threaded the ornaments with twine, take a round metal hoop and cover it with twine also, tying it off at the end. Use pegs to hold the twine in place as you do it. **(1)**

Hang the ornaments from the hoop at different heights. **(2)**

Tie four pieces of twine from the hoop and make a loop at the top so you can hang it up. **(3)**

Paper Clay Vase

I know you are going to look at this and say, "hold on, this takes more than an hour to make, surely". No, it doesn't. You can cut, wedge, imprint, roll and make this into a gorgeous vase in well under an hour. This will leave plenty of time for glazing. This is a very simple technique for making a vase.
These vases are not for water – they are rarely watertight. Instead, use them to display some gorgeous dried flowers or ornamental dried bamboos.

MATERIALS

- Big chunk of clay
- Rolling pin
- Fern fronds
- 30cm/1ft PVC piping
- Clay knife
- Newspaper

INSTRUCTIONS

Note: Before you begin this tutorial read the Using Paper Clay tutorial and follow the instructions for cutting, wedging and rolling the clay.

Roll out the clay until it is 1cm/⅜in. thick and a squarish shape. **(1)**

Place the fern fronds onto the clay and roll them into it. Remove the fronds and you are left with imprinted clay. **(2)**

Roll out another piece of clay until it is 2.5cm/1in. thick. Place the PVC piping onto the clay and cut around it, leaving an overlap of 1cm/⅜in.

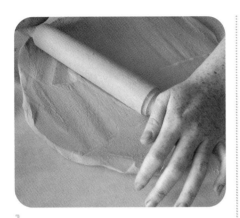

This will be the base of the vase. **(3)**

Cut the main piece of clay into a square by making the edges straight. **(4)**

Wrap the PVC piping in newspaper and stick it together with tape. **(5)**

Carefully turn the clay over so that the imprint is facing the bench. Roll the PVC piping up in the clay. Be gentle so that you don't smooth out the lovely frond imprints. **(6)**

Leave an overlap of about 2.5cm/1in. where the two edges meet up and cut off the excess clay with your knife. **(7)**

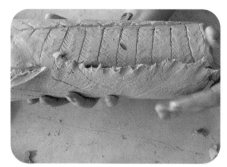

8

Press the overlap onto the other piece of clay. Tear the edges of the clay to make them look more rustic. **(8)**

Now stand up your vase and place it onto the round base. **(9)**

Cut away the excess clay on the base and blend the clay around the seam with your fingers. Leave the paper clay vase to dry for at least two days or until it is white and looks a little dusty. **(10)**

Follow the instructions in the Using Paper Clay tutorial to fire, glaze and fire your vase again. If you do not have a kiln to use, I suggest using a pottery store to fire it or a local potter's guild. They will fire your clay for a very small fee. **(11)**

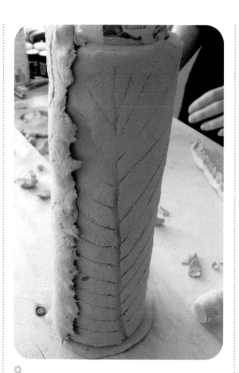

9

10

11

Decoupage Wall Art

Who would have thought that a few napkins and a bit of plaster could produce such vibrant and amazing wall art? I am always on the lookout now for new and interesting napkins to use. Instead of using napkins you could make a collage using Japanese lace papers or tissue papers. Flowers or other bright prints are really effective for this project.

MATERIALS

- Plaster of Paris (about 3 cups to make one tablet)

- Baking tin 23cm/8in. x 23cm/8inch

- Oxide colouring in limestone

- Baking paper

- Podge

- 2 crafting/decorative paper serviettes/napkins

- White acrylic paint

- Small piece of wire (like coathanger wire)

- Wire cutters

- Pliers

- Wooden spoon

- Paintbrush

- Old rag

- Emery paper

INSTRUCTIONS

Mix the plaster of Paris with water in a bucket. Follow the instructions on the packet you have bought. Add the oxide colour to the mix and stir well until all the lumps are out. **(1)** (Work quickly at this stage as the plaster of Paris begins to dry straight away.)

Line the tin with baking paper and pour the plaster of Paris into the tin. Use a spoon to make it level on top. **(2)**

Leave the plaster of Paris to harden for about 5 minutes. Cut a piece of wire 13cm/5in. long. Bend both ends at a right angle with your pliers. **(3)**

1

2

3

4

5

6

7

When the plaster is beginning to set, place the wire into it, 8cm/3in. from the top of the pan, in the middle. **(4)**

When the plaster is dry (10–15 minutes), remove the tablet from the pan and peel away the baking paper from the bottom. **(5)**

Paint the top of the tablet with white acrylic paint and leave it for a few minutes to dry. **(6)**

Cut two serviettes with the same picture to the size of the tablet. Peel the layers of both serviettes until you have only the top layer. **(7)**

Paint a layer of podge (decoupage paste) onto the tablet. Take the top layer of one serviette and gently stick

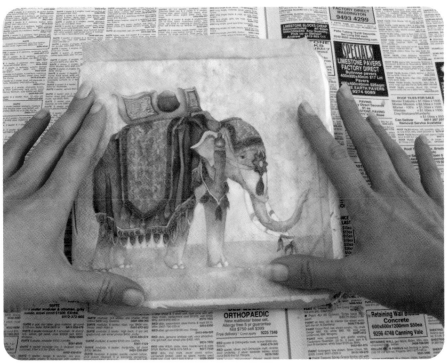

8

this to the tablet, smoothing it with your fingers. **(8)**

Apply another layer of podge, gently, to the top of the serviette. Now take the second serviette and make a few gentle tears in it. Place it on to the first and smooth it down with your fingers. **(9)**

9

10

11

Apply a final coat of podge on top.
Dry the podge with a hairdryer. **(10)**

With a rag, rub a thin layer of wood
stain onto the sides of the tablet. **(11)**

When the tablet is dry, take a small
piece of medium coarse sandpaper
and sand a thin line on the top edges
of the tablet, revealing some of the
white paint underneath. **(12)**

12

Polka Dot Drawer Handles

MATERIALS

- Polymer clay
- Drawer handles
- Rolling pin
- Lacquer
- Paintbrush

Polymer clay is a great medium to work with. It is very simple to use and can be cooked in your oven at home with no noxious fumes. It is versatile and safe to use. Before you use the clay, condition it by breaking off a piece and kneading it in your hands until it is soft and pliable. This will only take a few minutes. Once the clay is conditioned, it can be made into a million different things. These drawer handles are a great beginner project and an easy way to spruce up an old set of drawers or even a door knob.

1

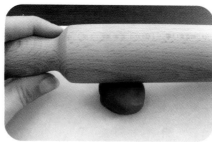

2

3

INSTRUCTIONS

Cut a square block of polymer clay, approximately 2cm/1in. **(1)**

Roll in the palm of your hands into a ball. Use a rolling pin to flatten out the clay into a flat disc approximately three times the size of the handle head. **(2, 3)**

Roll up small balls of light blue clay and arrange in a polka dot pattern over dark blue disc. **(4)**

Roll small balls into large disc **(5)**

Carefully peal off the disc from the board and turn upside down. **(6)**

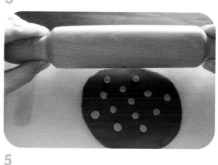

4

5

6

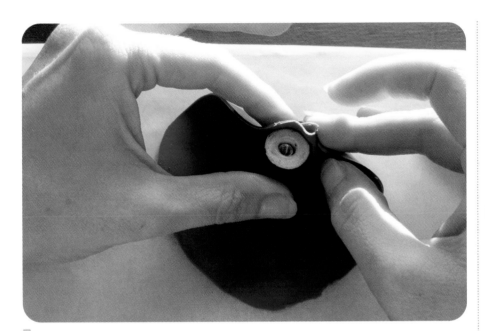

7

8

9

10

Place the handle in the middle of the disc and wrap the edges around the handle. **(7)**

Using a knife, trim off the excess clay so the edge is flush with the end of the handle. **(8)**

Place in preheated oven at 130°C/275°F for 20 minutes to harden the polymer clay (or follow the packet instructions). **(9)**

Paint a thin coat of lacquer onto the hardened clay and leave to dry. **(10)**

Mix and match, making more handles using different colour dots.

Polymer Clay Bottle Top

MATERIALS

- Four colours of polymer clay
- Hat pin (bought from a bead store)
- Crystal rondelle
- Small glass bead
- Water bottle
- Cork
- Hot glue gun
- Lacquer
- Small paintbrush
- Foil

These make a great addition to a really colourful dinner party table. This is a great way to start using polymer clay. These techniques provide you with the basic skills to make hundreds of variations. And of course, play around with different colour combinations to suit the style and occasion. I recommend using the same coloured bead on top as the water bottle, to help blend the colours.

INSTRUCTIONS

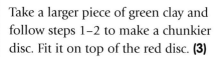

Take a small piece of clay. To soften it, roll it in your hands for a few minutes until it is warm. When it is warm, roll it into a ball between your palms. **(1)**

Take the ball and squash it into a disc shape. The disc should be just bigger than the cork. **(2)**

Take a larger piece of green clay and follow steps 1–2 to make a chunkier disc. Fit it on top of the red disc. **(3)**

Soften a piece of gold clay in your hands. Place it on the table and roll it into a long snake. Coil the snake on top of the green disk, pinching the top and bottom of it to make the coils flat at the ends. **(4)**

Roll another ball from the blue clay and fit this onto the top of the coil. **(5)**

6

7

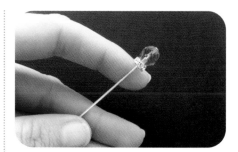

8

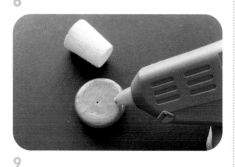

9

10

11

Push the hat pin into the top of the blue ball and right down to bottom of the red disc. Place this onto a piece of foil and put in an oven at 130°C/275°F for 20 minutes. Read and follow the instructions with your polymer clay as they could be different to these. **(6)**

Take the clay out of the oven and leave it to cool. Take the pieces from the hat pin, paint individually with a lacquer and leave to dry. **(7)**

Place the glass bead and rondelle onto the hat pin. **(8)**

Using your hot glue gun, glue the bottom of the red disc onto the top of the cork. **(9)**

Push all the clay pieces back onto the hat pin. Push the hat pin through the red disc and into the cork. **(10)**

Fill the bottles with water, oil, vinegar or a liquid of your choice and cork them with your lovely bottle tops. **(11)**

Painting, Printing and Etching

Abstract Miniature Paintings

Etched Bird Mirror

Stencilled Bird Tee

Abstract Miniature Paintings

If you are anything like me, you have been or are still terrified of painting. There seems to be something mystical about it. I am always scared of making mistakes. It's not like you can unpick it!

Here is a quick lesson to teach you to make a series of abstract paintings. When making these paintings, remember there is no wrong! My trick is to use foam brushes – I like the imperfection of it all. Another tip is to make three little paintings; they always look better en masse. Use bold colours which go well together. And finally, use the same idea with every pattern, just make it slightly different!

You can also use this method to make larger canvases to cover your living room walls! Just buy bigger foam brushes.

MATERIALS

- Acrylic paints in three bold colours (pink, yellow and blue)

- A foam brush with a long end

- A foam brush with a round end

- 3 little canvases

- Newspaper

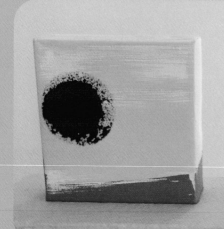

1

2

INSTRUCTIONS

Dip your foam brush into the paint and wipe the excess off onto the side of the bowl. Make a few sweeping strokes down the canvas on one side. Cover half of the canvas. Don't try to make it perfect. Paint the sides of the canvas in yellow in the areas where the canvas is yellow, leave the rest. **(1)**

Paint the other two canvases with the yellow paint using the same strokes. Cover different parts of the canvas in all three. Leave this paint to dry for ten minutes. **(2)**

3

4

Clean, and then dip the foam brush into the pink paint, and get rid of the excess. Another way to do this is to blot the brush onto newspaper. Now use a long stroke to paint pink paint onto the first canvas. Fill some of the white space on the canvas, but not all. **(3)**

Paint all the canvases with some pink paint. Make sure that each canvas is different. **(4)**

Leave these on a sheet to dry for ten minutes. **(5)**

Dip your round foam brush into the blue paint, blot the excess onto some paper and make one round form on the canvas. Repeat this on all three canvases. Now your paintings are finished **(6).** To seal your painting, apply a coat of spray-on varnish.

5

6

Etched Bird Mirror

The etched effect looks incredible. This is definitely one of my favourite things to do. When it is complete, the effect is eerily 3D.

MATERIALS

- Mirror (new or secondhand)
- Gloves
- Small craft knife
- Safety glasses
- Adhesive plastic (as used to cover books)
- Etching paste
- Bird image
- Small paintbrush
- Old cloth

Don't be scared of using etching paste but you must be really careful. It can be very dangerous! I recommend making sure that all small children are out of the house when you do this. Wear safety glasses and chemical-resistant gloves. Wear long sleeves, long trousers and covered shoes. Treat this chemical with respect and you will be fine. And you will quickly see the amazing results of your work!

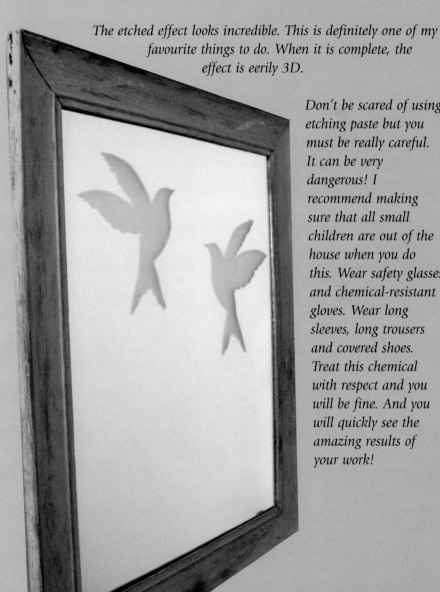

INSTRUCTIONS

Cut out two squares of the adhesive plastic – slightly larger than the bird image. Place the adhesive paper over the bird pattern and tape it to a window. Trace the bird outline onto the paper side of the contact sheet. **(1)** Turn the bird image over and repeat step two on the second piece of adhesive plastic.

Using the craft knife, carefully cut out the bird image from both pieces of the adhesive plastic. **(2)**

Remove the mirror from its frame and clean with soap and water, then re-clean and dry thoroughly. Once you have decided where to position the two birds on the mirror, carefully peel off the backing paper from the adhesive sheets and stick them into position. Ensure that all the inner edges of the bird stencils are smooth and stuck down well. **(3)**

1

2

With gloves and safety glasses on, and following all safety instructions on the etching paste jar, carefully paint the etching paste onto the bird stencil. Apply a thick, even layer of paste. Avoid getting any paste on the rest of the mirror. **(4)**

After 60 minutes (or according to the instructions on the jar), carefully and quickly wash off the paste in warm running water. Use plenty of water to thoroughly remove all traces of the paste. Wear your safety glasses and gloves. Refit the mirror frame and hang in a prominent location so everyone can admire your handiwork. **(5)**

3

4

5

Stencilled Bird Tee

I love using freezer paper to make stencils. This is American freezer paper. In countries outside USA, you can buy this from quilting and fabric stores.

I love using simple, bold designs. In a world busy with logos, brands and gaudiness, simple looks more effective. When you have used this image, find your own images on the internet or in books or magazines and make your own stencils. You could also make stencils with two or three colours. Make sure that each layer is dry before you paint the next layer. Why not put this design onto a plain linen skirt? I have stencilled cushions, bed covers, pyjamas, bags and skirts. Warning: this is a highly addictive craft.

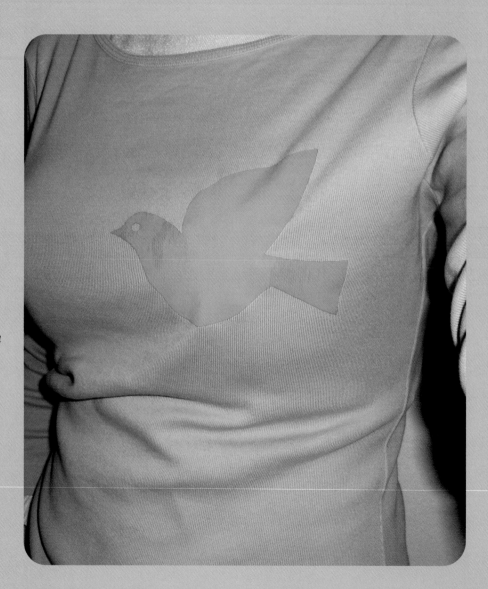

MATERIALS

- T-shirt – plain
- The Original Freezer Paper
- Fabric paint – pink
- Bird image
- Foam brush
- Small craft knife
- Cutting board
- Scissors
- Newspaper

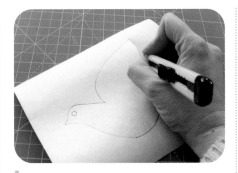

1

2

INSTRUCTIONS

Trace and carefully cut out the bird image from the freezer paper with your craft knife. **(1)**

Place the stencil onto the top left-hand side of the t-shirt with the shiny side down. Heat up the iron and iron it on for about two minutes. Make sure that the sides of the image are carefully ironed to the t-shirt, leaving no gaps. Cut out the eye piece and iron this on also. **(2)**

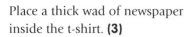

3

4

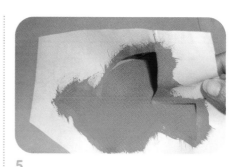

5

Place a thick wad of newspaper inside the t-shirt. **(3)**

Carefully paint the image. Fill all the edges with paint. Go gently over the eye piece. **(4)** When you have painted the whole image, hang the t-shirt in a warm place to dry for an hour or so.

When the paint is completely dry, pull away the stencil and the eye piece. **(5)** Iron the image with a cloth over it. Use a moderate iron for three minutes. This will make the image colourfast – this means that you can safely wash it and it will not be ruined.

Note: Wash separately for the first two washes.

Put on your stunning tee!

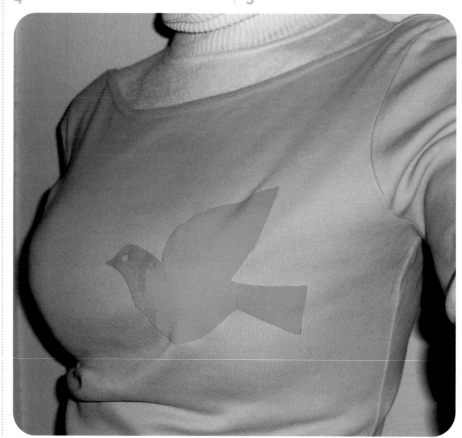

Jewellery

Chain Earrings

Chunky Bead Necklace

Japanese Paper Bangle

Three-tiered Necklace

Crystal Earrings

Chain Earrings

These are fun earrings to make and wear. Colourful, happy, they are easy enough for a beginner beader to make and interesting enough for someone who has been beading for a while, to throw together. I use very small beads in this tutorial so that the earrings are light to wear and don't drag your ears down or hurt. When you have chosen your outfit for Saturday night's party, why not whip up a pair.

MATERIALS

- 2 x 3cm/1.2in. silver twisted chain

- 2 silver earring backs

- 24 silver eye pins

- A pair of round-nosed pliers

- A pair of flat-nosed pliers

- A pair of wire cutters

- 24 large seed beads in assorted colours

INSTRUCTIONS

Sort out your seed beads into two identical piles of 12 beads each. Take an eye pin, place a seed bead onto it and use your wire cutters to cut it 1cm/⅜in. above the bead. **(1)** Repeat this with all 24 beads.

Make a small loop at the other end of the wire. Grab the wire's tip with your round-nosed pliers. Roll the wire to form a half circle. Release the wire. **(2)**

Position the pliers in the loop again and continue rolling, forming the circle above the bead. **(3)**

To centre the loop above the bead, hold the bead in the same way, remove the pliers from the loop and place them on the other side of the loop. Place the pliers on an angle and squeeze the bottom of the loop until it is centred. **(4)**

Repeat steps 2, 3 and 4 until you have used the 24 beads.

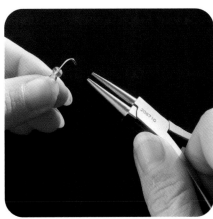

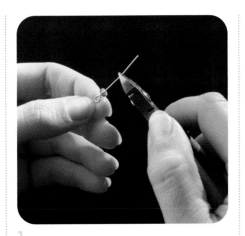

5

6

Take a bead and open the loop. Hold the bead between your fingers. Grasp one side of the loop with your flat-nosed pliers, and bring the pliers towards you. Repeat this step for all 24 beads. **(5)**

Attach the opened loop to the chain and close the loop with your flat-nosed pliers. Attach all 12 beads to one chain and then complete the other earring using the same pattern. **(6)**

7

Open the loop on an earring wire and slide the top chain link on to the loop. Close the loop. Repeat this to make the second earring. **(7)**

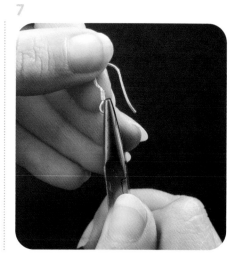

Chunky Bead Necklace

This necklace is so lovely it is almost edible. When I started making jewellery, I started making these fun necklaces. I made loads of them. In fact, most of my girlfriends and family own at least one.

These necklaces are so easy to make. They are a great way to start to learn to make lovely loops and to make neat joins with beaded jewellery. I recommend using silver-coated wire. I find sterling silver a little too soft to support these chunky glass beads without soldering the joints.

Play with colour. With this necklace, I used all forest colours, rich warm tones. Play with different shades of blue or green or try putting two colours that you would never normally wear together. Enjoy!

MATERIALS

- 16 silver-coated eyepins

- 18 10mm/⅜in. silver-coated jump rings

- 16 large, gorgeous chunky glass beads. Make sure that they are at least as big or a little bigger than the jump rings.

- Jewellery clasp

- Round-nosed pliers

- Flat-nosed pliers

- Wire cutters

1

2

3

4

INSTRUCTIONS

Choose your 16 beads (you may need more, depending on how long you want your necklace to be). Place a bead onto the eyepin. Cut the eyepin 1cm/⅜in. above the bead. **(1)**

With your round-nosed pliers, begin to roll the other end of the wire over. **(2)**

Re-position the pliers again and continue to roll the end into a loop. Place the pliers inside the loop and centre it. **(3)**

Repeat steps 1–3 for all 16 beads. Arrange the beads in the order you would like them. This is the time to experiment with different combinations. I used two of each bead to bring unity to the necklace,

5

6

7

but I didn't place them in a uniform pattern. **(4)**

Holding a jump-ring in your hand, open the jump ring to the side with your flat-nosed pliers. **(5)**

Place two loops from two beads onto the open jump ring. **(6)**

Close the jump ring using your flat-nosed pliers to bend it back into alignment. **(7)**

Join all the beads together with a jump ring in the middle. **(8)**

Open the loop on the jewellery clasp (in the same way you opened the jump ring) and attach it to one end of the necklace. Attach a jump ring to the other end, and join the clasp to the other end of the necklace. **(9)**

8

9

Japanese Paper Bangle

This bangle is easy and fun to make. I have made several of these and whenever I wear them, people comment. They look great en masse. Why not make a stack of these and pile them onto your arms? Experiment using different papers on the same bangle or using Japanese lace paper for a very different effect.

MATERIALS

- 1 plastic bangle

- 1 or 2 A4 pieces of Japanese paper

- Podge (decoupage paste)

- Small guillotine

- Scissors

- Emery paper

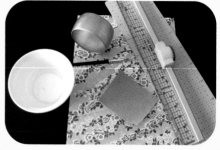

INSTRUCTIONS

Measure and cut strips of Japanese paper 2cm/¾in. wide with your guillotine. You can also use scissors. **(1)** Cut 20 pieces to begin with – you may need more.

Measure the pieces around your bangle. They need to be long enough to wrap around the whole bangle with a small overlap. Cut this to size. **(2)** Repeat this until you have cut all 20 pieces to the right size.

Cover a section of the outside of the bangle with podge. Starting from the outside, wrap the paper around the bangle. Paint podge in the middle of the bangle and stick the paper down. Glue down the overlapping paper. **(3)**

Now stick the other pieces of paper onto the bangle in the same way, overlapping each piece a little.

When you have covered the whole bangle, cut a long strip of paper, long enough to cover the inside of the bangle. Apply podge to the inside of the bangle and stick the paper around it. **(4)**

Cover the bangle with another layer of podge to varnish it and leave it in a warm place for a few hours to dry. **(5)**

Three-tiered Necklace

This looks like it would be hard to make, but it is so easy – friends and family will think you are a star, being able to construct this. I always believe in making life as easy as possible, which is why I suggest the use of eyepins in this tutorial. This alone will save you about twenty minutes in time. And that time could be spent having a catnap before going out to show off your necklace that night. And of course, experiment with different coloured and sized beads.

MATERIALS

- 2 jump rings
- 1 jewellery tag
- 1 lobster clasp
- 9 eyepins
- 3 large clear crystals
- 3 cone-shaped iron ore beads
- 3 large clear cubes
- Round-nosed pliers
- Square-nosed pliers
- Wire cutters

INSTRUCTIONS

Cut three lengths of chain 43cm/17in., 45cm/18in. and 50cm/20in. **(1)**

Take an eyepin, place a seed bead onto it and use your wire cutters to cut it 1cm/⅜in. above the bead. Repeat this with all nine beads. **(2)**

Make a small loop at the other end of the wire. Grab the wire's tip with your round-nosed pliers. Roll the wire to form a half circle. Release the wire. **(3)**

Position the pliers in the loop again and continue rolling, forming the circle above the bead. To centre the loop above the bead, hold the bead in the same way, remove the pliers from the loop and place them on the other side of the loop. Place the pliers at an angle and squeeze the bottom of the loop until it is centered. Repeat steps 2–4 until you have wired all nine beads. **(4)**

Lay the three chains in a row and work out where you would like to place the three beads on each row.

Make four snips in the first chain at these points and lay it out again on the table. Cut the second chain, placing the beads in between the

first. Cut the third chain, making sure that the cuts don't correspond to those in the other two chains. **(5)**

7

8

9

Hold a bead between your fingers. With your flat-nosed pliers, open the loop to the side. **(6)**

Take one of your lengths of chain and attach the opened bead to the end. Close the loop with your flat-nosed pliers. **(7)**

Open the other loop of the bead and attach it to the next piece of chain. **(8)**

Repeat steps 5–7 for all three beads and four chain lengths for the first strand. **(9)**

Attach all the beads to the remaining two lengths of chain in the same way. **(10)**

10

11

To attach the jewellery tag and lobster clasp, pass each of them through a jump ring and attach each jump ring to opposite ends of the chains. **(11)**

Crystal Earrings

(How to Make Your Own Earring Wires)

If you are like me, you long for findings, particularly for earrings which have minimal fuss and smooth lines. The answer? Make your own earring wires. These are just simply elegant and so easy to make. If you have never used pliers before and are not used to bending wire buy a roll of silver-plated wire to practice with.

MATERIALS

- A pair of round-nosed pliers

- A pair of flat-nosed pliers

- Wire cutters

- 2 Silver or gold jewellery pins gauge 24 or higher

- 2 crystals of your choice. For this project I bought flat crystals but I have also used round crystals and they look lovely too.

- A small piece of emery paper

INSTRUCTIONS

Push a crystal onto the end of a jewellery pin. **(1)**.

Hold the crystal with wire parallel to your table, between your thumb and forefinger. Now bend the wire at a right angle to the bead. If your wire is not soft, you may need to use your pliers to complete these steps. **(2)**.

Leave about 1cm/⅜ in. of straight wire, then take the round pliers. Using the largest end of the pliers, bend the wire back on itself. Make sure that both wires are parallel to each other. Leave a 1.5cm/⅝in. length of wire at the back and then cut the end from the wire. **(3)**

Take the round pliers and gently bend the bottom tip of the wire outwards in a gentle slope. **(4)**

Rip off a small piece of fine emery paper and gently sand the bottom tip of the wire to take off any burrs or sharp edges. Only spend a minute or so doing this. **(5)**

1

2

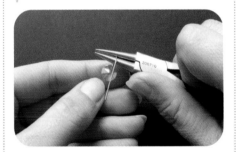

3

4

5

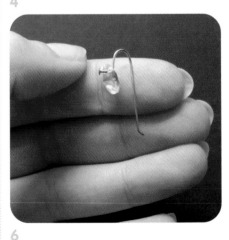

6

Voila a very simple sexy pair of earrings! **(6)**

Plastic

CD and Spoon Clock

Heart Shoe Bling

Suncatcher

Plastic Keyring or Bag Dangle

Button Magnets

CD and Spoon Clock

I love this clock. It is so cute and looks very cool on the wall and the best part of all for me – it is just so easy to put together. Once you have made one, you can experiment with using other things than utensils. You could also use an old record instead of a CD.

Fire up your hot glue gun and begin the fun!

MATERIALS

- 1 CD (this is a good way to recycle an old CD)

- 12 coloured plastic utensils – e.g. 4 knives, 4 spoons and 4 forks

- I clock movement

- I packet of clock hands

- Hot glue gun

- Marker pen that writes on CD's

- Ruler

- Protractor

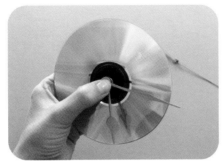

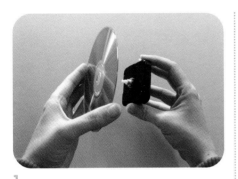

INSTRUCTIONS

Attach the back of the clock mechanism by pushing it through the hole in the CD. **(1)**

Press the clock hands onto the front of the clock mechanism. Follow the instructions on the clock mechanism packet. **(2)**

Place all the clock hands at the same point on the CD face. Using a marker put a small line on the back or front of CD to mark this as your number twelve. **(3)**

Rotate the hands around the clock face, until the big hand reaches the number twelve. The little hand will now be at one o'clock. Put a mark on the CD to make one o'clock. Continue to move the hands around the clock face in the same way, until you have marked each hour on the clock. **(4)**

Heat up your glue gun. Place a dab of glue onto a spoon and press the spoon onto the CD at the first mark. Continue to glue the spoons onto the CD face at all the points you have marked. **(5)**

Place a battery in the clock, set the time and hang it onto the wall.

Heart Shoe Bling

When I discovered that you could easily melt Pony Beads to make things, I was intrigued. Then when I thought up this idea and it turned out as stunning as I had imagined, I was over the moon. Clip these onto your shoes. Note: The fumes are very noxious. Make sure that the area is well ventilated. I opened up the windows and put the kitchen fan on.

MATERIALS

- Red, black and purple pony beads
- Heart-shaped cookie cutter
- Foil
- Cooking tray
- File/emery paper
- 2 clip-on earring backs
- Tweezers
- Hot glue gun

1

2

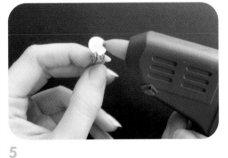

3

4

5

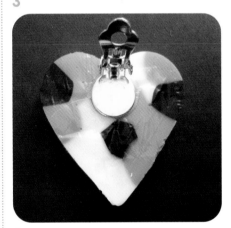

6

INSTRUCTIONS

Line the cooking tray with foil, and place the cookie cutter onto the foil. Using the tweezers pick up and place a layer of pony beads into the cookie cutter. Leave the holes facing upwards, so you don't get air bubbles when you melt them. **(1)**

Carefully place a few more beads on top of the first layer, particularly where you see holes. I placed two purple beads only, as accents. **(2)**

Cook the beads in the oven at 220C/430F for about 15 minutes. Take the tray out of the oven when the beads have melted. Put the tray under cold water for a few minutes and when it is cool, push the heart out of the cutter. **(3)**

Lightly file, then emery the edges of the heart. Do not try and get all the lumps and bumps out of the plastic. It will take you hours and will not look as organic and gorgeous. **(4)**

Heat up your hot glue gun. Place a large dab of glue onto the earring back. **(5)** Turn your heart over so that the right side is facing the table. Place the earring back with the glue onto the heart, just below the indent, in the middle top. Hold the back in place until the glue dries. **(6)** When you have made both clips, snap them onto a pair of sassy shoes.

Suncatcher

This suncatcher has a retro, psychedelic vibe to it. It also reminds me of kaleidoscopes from my childhood. You can also use this on your kitchen table to put a dish or vase on. These are so easy to make. In fact if you are really adventurous, you can take this plate and slump it to make a vase. Just place this plate on top of an empty soft drink can and place on a baking tray. Put it in the oven for a few minutes; it only takes about five minutes to slump.

Note: before you do this project, open the windows and turn on all the fans. The fumes are noxious!

MATERIALS

- Round baking tin (in the size you want)

- A large bag of opaque pony beads (available at any craft store, they are very inexpensive)

- Small bag of see-through pony beads

- Small bowls

- Dremmel drill with small tip

- Fishing line

INSTRUCTIONS

Spend a few minutes and sort the beads into bowls of the same colour or similar colours such as yellows

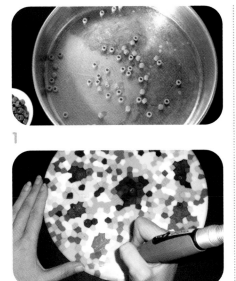

1

2

3

4

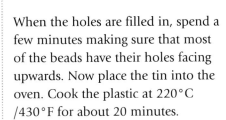

5

6

and oranges together. Scatter one bowl of pony beads into the baking tin. Try to spread these as evenly as possible. **(1)**

Continue to scatter the beads, one bowl at a time into the tin. **(2)**

Place the see-through beads into the tin in groups, making a deliberate, regular pattern. Place a few of these beads into the centre of the tin. Fill in any gaps with leftover beads. **(3)**

When the holes are filled in, spend a few minutes making sure that most of the beads have their holes facing upwards. Now place the tin into the oven. Cook the plastic at 220°C /430°F for about 20 minutes.

When all the beads are melted take the tin out of the oven and run under a cold tap for a few minutes. When the tin is cool, remove the plate from the tin.

Mark a point with a pen near one edge. Place your plate on a piece of

wood and drill your hole carefully with your Dremmel drill. **(4)**

Cut a piece of fishing line the length you require, thread it through the hole on the plate and tie the two ends into a double knot. **(5)**

Hang the suncatcher in a tree or in a window. Make sure that it is a place where the sun will shine through. **(6)**

Plastic Keyring or Bag Dangle

These are so easy to make and a great way to use extra knick-knacks you have around the house. If you don't have knick-knacks, raid the kid's rooms for little plastic figurines or pieces of lego. Craft and toy shops contain an endless number of these knick-knacks, so keep an eye out for miniature pens, pencils and oddments. When making your bag dangle, you could choose a theme to stick to. If you are going on a girls' weekend, get everyone to buy one knick-knack then make the dangles, with a special momento for each person of the weekend.

MATERIALS

- Keyring clasp

- Flat-nosed jewellery pliers

- 2 lengths of plastic tubing (also known as Scoubidoo)

- Assorted buttons, plastic tokens, plastic beads, glass beads, 2 metal charms, mini peg, mini pen or other knick-knacks.

- Small pieces of ribbon

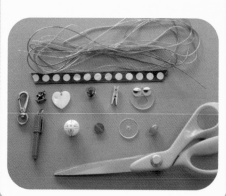

INSTRUCTIONS

Fold one length of plastic tubing in half and double knot it around the loop of the keyring clasp. **(1)**

Slip a glass foil bead onto one side of tubing, about 3cm/1in. down and tie a single knot under it. Knot two or three trinkets on each side of the tubing and tie a knot under it. **(2, 3)**

Repeat step 1 two times so that you have all three plastic tubes attached to the keyring clasp. **(4)** Add all the beads to them as in step 2. **(5)**

Cut a piece of ribbon or lace 15cm /6in. and knot it to the loop of the keyring clasp as well. **(6)**

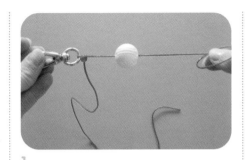

1

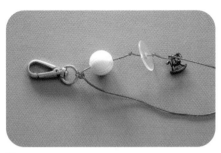

2

3

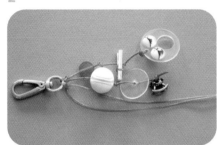

4

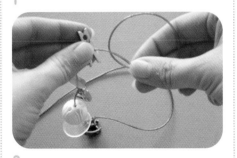

5

6

Button Magnets

This really is five minute craft! These literally take five minutes to whip up. What a great present to make – something that is cute, useful and can be made so quickly. I love these sort of crafts. If you take care with these and package them in a little vintage tin or a little silver tin, they make lovely gifts. For Christmas I ended up making well over a hundred of these and packaged them twelve to a tin. I then gave them to people I wanted to say thank you to for something they had done for me over the year.

MATERIALS

- Vintage buttons – as many as you plan to make.

- Little round magnets (available from craft stores)

- Hot glue gun

- Little vintage tin

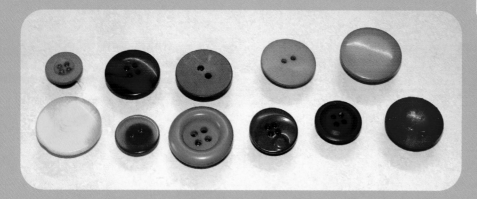

INSTRUCTIONS

Heat up the hot glue gun for a few minutes until the glue comes easily out of the end.

Take a magnet and using your hot glue gun, make a circle of glue around the outside of it. **(1)**

Quickly press the button into the glue and hold for about twenty seconds. **(2)**

Place the magnet somewhere and leave to dry.

Try all sorts of colour combinations. When you place the buttons into the little tin you have chosen, it is amazing to see which colours go together.

Half the fun for me with making these little gems is hunting around in thrift stores for vintage buttons and little tins. You can find the most amazing old buttons to use.

Garden

Teacup and Saucer Bird Feeder

Feng Shui Pebble Plaque

Flower Teapot

Succulent Moon

Heart Wind Chime

Teacup and Saucer Bird Feeder

MATERIALS

- 2 teacups and saucers (mine were bought from a charity shop)
- 1 wood plank 7.5cm/3in. wide and at least 31cm/12in.
- 2.5m/8ft of 1.6mm/⅟₁₆in. thick galvanized chain
- 8 hoop nails
- 1 split ring (you can take one from a keyring)
- Constructive adhesive glue
- Blue spray paint
- Drill
- Hammer
- Bird seed

What a cute, quirky bird feeder for the garden. So, "get out of bed and get a hammer and nails. There is nothing more rewarding than spending an hour or two outside, getting some fresh air at the same time as making a fun and funky piece of craft. I felt especially clever designing and making this – and I am sure you will too!

INSTRUCTIONS

Measure and saw the wood plank into two lengths of wood 16.5cm/6.5in. long. **(1)**

Measure and cut four pieces of chain, 50cm/20in. long. **(2)**

Nail the end loops of the four pieces of chain to the corners (on the longer outseide edges) of one piece of wood. **(3)**

When all the chains have been nailed to the first piece of wood, measure the point 17cm/8in. up the chains. At this point, attach the chains to the corners of the second piece of wood. Nail these in same way as the first piece of wood. **(4)**

Now that your two pieces of wood are joined by the chains, link the remaining chain together at the top with the split ring. Loop another 40cm/16in. chain in half and attach this to the split ring. **(5)**

Spray paint the bird feeder and chain and hang it to dry. When this is dry, glue the saucers to the wood and the cups to the saucers. **(6)**

Fill the cups with bird seed and hang the bird feeder by the chain onto a tree in the garden. Wait and watch as the birds come and enjoy the seed! **(7)**

Feng Shui Pebble Plaque

I have called this a Feng Shui Plaque because I discovered that the different coloured river stones all have powerful meaning in Feng Shui. The black stones help to attract wealth, prosperity and power into your life. The pink stones help you to be sensitive and understanding. The white stones bring purity and cleansing to your home. This is another great project for a sunny morning spent outdoors.

MATERIALS

- Piece of exterior plywood 9mm thick. Cut the piece to measure 43cm/17in. by 30cm/12in.

- 3 x 1.5kg/3.3 lbs bags of river pebbles in black, white and pink

- Constructive adhesive glue

- Brown tiling grout

- Gardening gloves

- Old rags

- Plastic bucket

- Wooden spoon

1

INSTRUCTIONS

Have the wood cut to the specified size at your local hardware store. Or you can saw it yourself.

Using all the pebbles, make your pattern on a piece of cardboard the same size as your wood. I started the pattern by making a line of pebbles on each end. Then I decided to make a circle of pebbles in the middle. I then made larger circles around and ended up filling in the gaps. **(1)**

When you are happy with your pattern, begin glueing the pebbles onto the wood. Squeeze a zigzag line of glue onto one end and then transfer the pebbles from your

2

3

cardboard, pressing them firmly into the glue . **(2)**

Complete each section of the board by laying down the glue then transferring the pebbles, pressing each one down firmly. **(3)**

4

5

6

7

8

9

When you have finished, leave the constructive adhesive to dry for a few minutes. If any pebbles are loose, re-glue them. **(4)**

Mix up the tiling grout in a bucket (according to the instructions on the packet). **(5)**

Take handfuls of grout and smooth it over the pebbles. Makre sure you

cover it well and press the grout smoothly and firmly into the gaps between the pebbles. **(6)**

Cover the sides of the board with a medium layer of grout. **(7)**

Wipe away as much excess grout as you can with an old rag and leave the plaque to dry for the night. **(8)**

Wet your rag and wipe away any dust

and extra grout from the surface of the pebbles. Attach some wire to the back of the plaque and hang it on a wall in your garden or prop it in a special corner or niche in your garden. **(9)**

Flower Teapot

I love this pretty idea for growing flowers. What better than teapots to grow them in? Gorgeous old teapots can be found at local charity shops. A whole line of teapots around a front or back door or on a window sill looks delightful. You could also fill them with herbs and make your own little teapot herb garden.

MATERIALS

- Ceramic or clay teapot
- Cordless drill
- Masonry drill bits, small, medium and large
- Safety glasses
- Flower potting compost
- A small handful of stones
- Gardening gloves
- Glass scorer
- Flowers
- Marker

INSTRUCTIONS

Turn your teapot upside down and mark the places for holes on the bottom. You will need about five holes. **(1)**

Mark the spot for the holes with an indent using a glass scorer. **(2)**

Place the small drill bit into your drill and holding your drill upright and over the first indent, begin to slowly drill a hole. When you have made a small hole, change the drill bit and replace it with a medium drill bit. Drill into the same hole, slowly, making it larger. Change the drill bit again to a larger size and drill again into the same hole. Repeat this process to make four holes in the bottom of the teapot. Doing it gradually like this should prevent the teapot from cracking or shattering. **(3)**

Place a handful of stones into the bottom of the pot for drainage and fill up the teapot with potting mix nearly to the top. **(4)**

1

2

3

4

Take one of your flowers out of its pot. Gently loosen the soil around its roots. Make a hole with your fingers in the potting mix and plant the flower in it. Plant one or two more flowers, depending on the size of your pot. **(5)**

Water the flowers gently and place them in a sunny spot to grow!

5

Succulent Moon

I went to a garden show last year and was taken aback by a succulent ball, a completely round ball covered in succulents. I thought it to be perhaps the most beautiful garden idea I had ever seen. I then came home and spent a long time adapting this idea to be a one hour craft. And the results I believe are just as stunning! This is a little fiddly to make and I found that four hands were much better than two, so if possible enlist the help of your partner or lucky friend.

MATERIALS

- Variety of succulents (found at your local garden centre)

- Gardening gloves

- Thin steel garden wire

- Wire cutters

- Crescent shaped basket with lining

- Bag of succulent potting compost

- Sphagnum moss

1

2

3

4

5

INSTRUCTIONS

Remove a succulent plant from its pot and discard all the soil. Be careful not to damage the roots. **(1)**

Gently push a 25cm/10in. length of thin garden wire through the succulent stem. **(2)**

Carefully wrap the wire around the stem to secure it. **(3)**

Place the wired succulent onto the outside of the basket with the roots sitting inside the basket. Feed the tail end of the wire through to the back of the basket and secure the wire to the other side of the basket. **(4)**

Repeat steps 1–4 until you have covered the whole crescent of the basket.

Hang the basket onto a wall and pack sphagnum moss behind all of the plants. **(6)**

Cut and fit the basket lining into the back of the basket. **(7)**

With the lining in place and all the holes filled with sphagnum moss, fill the whole basket with succulent potting mix and water. **(8)**

Cover the top of the basket with lining and secure in place with two to three lengths of wire, by running the wire from the top of the front edge to the top of the rear edge and twisting the wire around each edge. **(9)**

Turn the basket upside down so that the planted crescent is on the top and hang it in a prominent sunny location on a wall or fence. **(10)**

6

7

8

9

10

Heart Wind Chime

This appeals to the gypsy in all of us. I love a garden full of colour and unpretentious bits and pieces, ecclectic and lovely. If you don't want to make a heart, try making a diamond shape or a star.

MATERIALS

- 140cm/53in. thick tin wire (like coat hanger wire)

- 50cm/20in. chicken wire

- 260cm/102in. thinner tin wire

- 50cm/20in. galvanized 9mm chain

- Pliers

- Wire cutters

- Round-nosed jewellery pliers

- Flat-nosed jewellery pliers

- 26 silver and gold bells

- 20 colourful glass beads

INSTRUCTIONS

Cut a piece of thick wire, 140cm/53in. long. **(1)**

Cut a piece of chain 50cm/20in. long. You can change the length of the chain to suit where you are going to hang the wind chime. **(2)**

Fold the chain in half and thread both ends onto the wire. **(3)**

Push the chain to the middle of the wire. Make a small loop in the wire with your pliers to hold the chain in place. Twist the end of the loop a few times to keep it in place. **(4)**

Take the two ends of the wire and twist them together, three or four times to hold them in place. This twist becomes the bottom of the heart. Form the wire shape into a heart with your hands, trying to make it as even as possible on both sides. **(5)**

Place your wire heart on top of your chicken wire and cut around it, leaving a 2.5cm/1in. allowance on all sides. **(6)**

Twist the stray edges of the chicken wire around the wire heart with your pliers. You may need to trim more of the excess chicken wire to neatern up the edges. **(7)**

Cut 26 8cm/3.5in. lengths of the thin wire. Bend them in half, put a bell on each and twist both wire ends around the chicken wire. Repeat this and spread them evenly throughout the spaces. **(8)**

Cut ten lengths of thin wire, each 5cm/2in. long. Make a loop on one end of each, using the round-nosed pliers. Place two beads on the wire and attach the wire to the chicken wire by looping and twisting it. Repeat this for all the glass beads. **(9)**

Hang your wind chime from a tree and listen to it tinkle in the wind.

6

7

8

9

Day Spa

Sand Candles

Avocado Mask

Tingly Yogurt and Honey Facial Cleanser

Popsicle Soaps

Oatmeal Scrub Soap

Sand Candles

These candles are rustic and lovely. They look gorgeous outdoors or in, particularly around the bath. To make the different colour shades, I made one candle at a time mixing different amounts of red and yellow. You could do this really well with blue and yellow dyes as well to get candles across the blue and green spectrum. You could also use a square tin to make the candle shape or a heart-shaped tin. Just make sure you pack the sand into the bowl really well before making your indent.

MATERIALS

- Wax – buy chunks or about six new candles

- Solid wax dye chunks

- Candle wicking

- Casserole dish or other dish

- Smaller, round bottomed dish

- Small bag of washed, white sand

- Double saucepan or a bowl inside a saucepan (use your worst saucepan or this gets messy)

- Wooden spoon

- Scissors

INSTRUCTIONS

Pour white sand into your casserole dish until it is two-thirds filled. Level the sand on top. Make a hole in the sand with your fist. **(1)**

Take the smaller dish and push it into the hole, making it larger. Make

1

2

3

the hole as big as you would like the candle to be. Level the sand on outside of the dish. **(2)**

To work out how much wax you need, break up your candles and fill the small bowl with the wax, adding a little extra. **(3)**

Measure and cut a piece of wicking which reaches from the top to the bottom of the hole, plus 10cm. Tie one end of the wick onto a wooden spoon or stick. Dangle the wick into the middle of the hole until it reaches the bottom. **(4)**

Melt your wax in a double saucepan on a low heat. Stir it slowly. Make sure your wax doesn't burn; you want to just melt it. **(5)**

Grate some dye and mix it into the melted wax with a wooden spoon.

4

6

5

Pour the melted wax gently into the hole in the sand, making sure that the wick stays in the middle. **(6)**

Leave the candle to harden. It may take a few hours.

7

When the candle is dry, remove it from the sand, dust off the excess and display on a plate. **(7)**

Avocado Mask

This face mask is very easy to make and leaves for skin soft and supple. It stores nicely in the fridge for a week – or maybe even two. I have made up some before a girls' night in at my house. Invite your closest freinds, cook some delicious food, and sit and watch your favourite TV programmes whilst indulging in this great beauty treatment. Who knew that a face mask could be so fun?

MATERIALS

- Medium-sized ripe avocado
- 2 dessertspoons avocado oil
- 1 dessertspoon calendula oil
- 1 cup Fuller's Earth
- 2 tablespoons rosewater (add a little more if you want the clay to be lighter)

INSTRUCTIONS

Mash the avocado with a fork in a bowl until smooth. **(1)**

Slowly add the sifted clay to the mixture, stirring well to make it into a paste. **(2)**

Add the avocado oil, a few drops at a time. Add the calendula oil in the same way. **(3)**

Stir in the rosewater to make the consistency thinner. **(4)**

When the mask is smooth and lovely, place it into an airtight container and store in the fridge. **(5)**

When you are ready to use the mask, put it on your face with your fingertips for twenty minutes. Lie on the couch and take it easy. Then wash it off with warm water.

1

2

3

4

5

Tingly Yoghurt and Honey Facial Cleanser

This recipe is for all skin types. I have very sensitive skin and I played around with the recipe so that it tingles a little on my skin but did not cause an allergic reaction. And apart from the cat jumping onto the table and sticking his head into the mixture as I was making it, this has not been tested on animals. The yoghurt and oil leaves your skin soft. I prefer to use this cleanser and swear that it is better for my skin than the expensive skincare products available for a good chunk of your monthly salary at a department store.

MATERIALS

- 2 tablespoons plain yoghurt
- 1 teaspoon wheatgerm oil
- 2 tablespoons clear honey
- 2 tablespoons rosewater
- 1 teaspoon lemon juice
- 1 teaspoon lemon rind
- 1 tablespoon flour

INSTRUCTIONS

Mix together the yoghurt, wheatgerm oil and honey in a bowl. **(1)**

Add the rosewater and stir well. **(2)**

Cut and squeeze a fresh lemon half into the mixture. **(3)**

Grate a teaspoon of lemon rind into the mixture. **(4)**

Sift the flour into the mixture and blend it together until it is smooth and milky. **(5)**

Apply the mixture to your face with your fingers, rub into your skin. Remove with warm water.

Cover the remaining mixture and store it in the fridge. Use twice a day.

1

2

3

4

5

Popsicle Soaps

When I was thinking about making soaps for this book, I wanted them to be different and fun. After a day of playing around in the kitchen with many different ideas, my daughter and I came up with this idea. These four soaps will take you about half an hour to make!

MATERIALS

- 500g/1.1lb of clear Melt and Pour Soap (enough to fill all popsicle wells)

- Four-hole popsicle tray

- Mixing bowl and spoon

- Alcohol rub or methanol in a spray bottle

- Food colouring (four different colours)

- Coloured pop sticks

- Essential oil – I used lavender and orange for these

INSTRUCTIONS

Chop up the Melt and Pour Soap (enough to fill one popsicle well) and melt in the microwave. **(1)**

Add 5 drops of both your essential oil and yellow food colouring to your melted soap. **(2)**

Pour one quarter of your coloured soap liquid into each of the popsicle tray wells. **(3)**

Repeat steps 1–3 above for each of your remaining three colours, spraying a small amount of alcohol rub or methanol between each layer.

When all the wells are filled, place pop sticks into each and allow to set in the fridge or in a cool, dry location. **(4)**

1

2

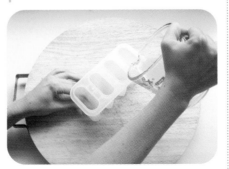
3

4

Oatmeal Scrub Soap

I love the look of this funky soap. It is great as an exfoliant in the shower, but is not too scratchy. It will leave your skin soft and glowing. These make great presents also. Wrap each soap in paper and package in a gorgeous little box. Or use when guests come to stay. And they are so quick to make.

MATERIALS

- 1 cup Melt and Pour Soap (opaque)
- ⅓ cup rolled oats
- ½ cup Clay (brown or white)
- Blue food colouring
- Ylang Ylang essential oil

1

2

3

INSTRUCTIONS

Place the Melt and Pour Soap into a jug and melt in the microwave. (You need to work fast with the ingredients after you have melted the Melt and Pour Soap because it hardens quite quickly).

Add the oats, clay and five drops of essential oil. **(1)**

Add five drops of blue food colouring. **(2)**

Quickly mix together into a smooth paste. **(3)**

Roll some of the soap into balls between your hands for a rough look. Place some soaps in little pots to solidify for a smoother surface.

Food

Banana Bread

Chocolate Chip Cookies in a Jar

Florentines

Tomato Relish

Banana Bread

A few years ago I started baking bread in little plant pots, with the baking paper and the bread bulging out over the top. It was amazing. I discovered that there are a lot more ways to cook bread than just in a traditional pan. For this bread I divided the mixture into three tins, actually baked beans tins, lined them and filled them with the mixture. These make particularly good presents to take to a friend's house when you drop in for tea or to leave as a little present. I added chocolate chips to this recipe because I am a chocoholic with no urge to break the habit. Sultanas would also taste delicious in this bread.

MATERIALS

- 3 ripe bananas
- 2 tablespoons melted butter
- 200g/6½oz brown sugar
- 1 egg
- 15ml/½floz milk
- 125g/4oz self-raising flour
- ¾ cup chocolate chips

INSTRUCTIONS

Peel the bananas and mash them with a fork in the mixing bowl. **(1)**

Turn your oven on now to pre-heat to 180°C/350°F.

Add the melted butter, brown sugar and egg to the bowl. Give it a quick stir. **(2)**

Add the milk and self-raising flour to the bowl. Now mix it for two minutes with an electric mixer (or by hand if you don't own one). Make sure it is well mixed and all big lumps are gone. **(3)**

Fold the chocolate chips into the mixture with a wooden spoon. **(4)**

Grease a tin with butter and line with baking paper. Spoon the mixture into the tin until it is two-thirds full. Bake the bread in the preheated oven for 35minutes at 180°C/350°F.

Allow the bread to cool for ten or more minutes. **(5)**

Tip out the bread and slice. Watch it disappear!

As a variation you can also add sultanas to the mixture.

Chocolate Chip Cookies in a Jar

MATERIALS

- 2 cups plain flour
- 1 teaspoon salt
- 1 teaspoon baking soda
- 150g/5oz brown sugar
- 170g/5¼ozwhite sugar
- 100g/3½oz choc chips
- 1 cookie jar
- Cardboard
- Twine or ribbon

I was originally given this as a present from a girlfriend and thought it was a lovely idea. There is so much joy in placing a batch of cookies in the oven and having the smell waft around the house. It also means that the recipient can keep the jar until they are in the mood for cookies. Why not make a few jars and keep them ready for you or your children to whip them up on a rainy day. Baking them yourself will be much more satisfying and saves a trip to the shops to buy the branded varieties which may contain all sorts of additives and preservatives in them. And these taste divine!

INSTRUCTIONS

Sift the flour, salt and baking soda into a bowl and pour into the jar. Level off the top with a spoon. **(1)**

Measure and carefully pour the brown sugar into the jar, so it lies in a neat layer on top of the flour. **(2)**

Add the white sugar to the jar in another neat layer and scatter in the choc chips as the top layer. **(3)**

Take a piece of card and fold in half. In the middle write the instructions to make the cookies. Tie the card around the jar with a pretty ribbon or a rustic piece of twine. **(4)**

What to write on the card….
Dear Friend,
Here's how to make your delicious cookies.
Pour the contents of the jar into a bowl.
Add 1 cup softened butter.
Add 1 egg, slightly beaten.
Add 1 teaspoon vanilla essence.
Bake for 8–10 minutes at 190°C/375°F.
Enjoy!

1

2

3

4

Florentines

I love these biscuits with coffee. They look so pretty all packaged in a little box with layers of baking paper in between. If you want to make mini Florentines, make sure that you crush the cornflakes in the bowl, chop the cherries into small pieces and place smaller spoonfuls onto the tray. However, I usually prefer them gorgeous and chunky.

MATERIALS

- 160g/6oz sultanas
- 80g/13oz flaked almonds
- 70g/12.5oz shredded coconut
- 165g/6oz glace cherries halved
- 80g/3oz crushed cornflakes
- 1 tin (375ml) condensed milk
- 100g/3.5oz cooking chocolate
- Baking paper
- Gift box

INSTRUCTIONS

Mix the sultanas, flaked almonds, coconut and cherries in a bowl. Add a tin of condensed milk. **(1)**

1

2

3

Mix in all the remaining ingredients and mix together with a wooden spoon. **(2)**

Place a sheet of baking paper onto a baking tray. Place spoonfuls of the mixture onto a tray and pat it down with the spoon until you have formed round biscuits. Their shape will not change much when being cooked. **(3)** Place in an oven at 180°C/350°F for eight minutes.

Remove the Florentines from the oven when they are a little golden on top. Leave them on a cooling rack for about 20 minutes. **(4)**

Place the chocolate into a bowl and microwave for two minutes on a low heat. Take the bowl from the microwave and stir gently with a spoon. Place it back in the microwave on low heat for another two minutes.

4

5

6

7

Take the Florentines from the cooling rack and turn them over so that the flat side is facing upwards. Place a spoonful of melted chocolate onto the Florentine and spread it around with the bottom of the spoon. **(5)**

Take a fork and make waves through the chocolate. **(6)**

Line a gift box with baking paper and place the Florentines inside for the perfect gift. **(7)**

Tomato Relish

I intended for all the foods in this book to be great as presents, and relish is no exception. There is no stove hovering required which is great. You just need to stay in the general vicinity, really. This recipe makes four little jars of relish or two big jars. Double the recipe to make enough to give for presents at Christmas. While the relish is cooking, I spend the time cutting out circles from fabric to place on the top of the jar, collecting ribbon and raffia to tie around it, making little cards to tie around the jars and sterilising the jars. Then when a birthday or occasion comes, I have these all ready to go.

MATERIALS

- 1kg/2lb 4oz tomatoes
- 1 small apple
- 375ml vinegar
- 225g/8oz sugar
- 2 small onions
- 1 clove garlic
- 1 tablespoon salt
- ½ dessertspoon mustard powder
- ½ dessertspoon curry powder
- 1 dessertspoon cornflour

1

2

3

INSTRUCTIONS

Chop the tomatoes into small cubes.
(1) Peel the apple and chop into
small pieces. **(2)** Chop the onions
into small pieces. **(3)**

Place the chopped tomatoes, apple
and onions, plus all the remaining
ingredients into a medium sized
saucepan. **(4)**

Stir together all the ingredients. Put a
lid on the saucepan and place it on a
high heat until it begins to simmer. **(5)**

Turn the heat down to a low simmer
and leave to cook for an hour and a
half with the lid on. If you need more
liquid in the pot, add a cup of water.
After an hour, turn off the heat and

4

5

leave the relish to cool. Sterilise your
jars by placing them in the microwave
on high for two minutes. **Note: Please
consult your microwave oven
guidelines, as heating an empty bowl
may be dangerous. If you are not
sure then add a small amount of
water.** Spoon the relish into the jars. **(6)**

Decorate the jars with labels, fabric
and wrap with ribbons to make great
presents.

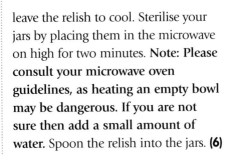

6

Index